If I Was Organized, I'd Be A Librarian

Organizational Tips From A Librarian

Dale Carpenter

Copyright 2014 by Dale Carpenter

All rights reserved. No part of this book, except for brief passages in articles and reviews that credit both author and publisher, may be stored or reproduced by any means without express written permission from the author.

LIES TOLD PRESS, LTD.

Published by Lies Told Press, Ltd., Non-fiction Division
P.O. Box 14, Rockaway, New Jersey 07866

Printed in the United States of America.

Carpenter, Dale
    If I Was Organized, I'd Be A Librarian: Organizational Tips From A Librarian.

Bibliography
Includes index.
1. Organization skills.　　　　　2. Life skills.

640 CAR　　　　　　　　　TX158.C434
ISBN 978-0-9631910-5-2

The author and publisher shall have neither liability nor responsibility to any person or entity with respect to any loss or damage caused, or alleged to be caused, directly or indirectly by the information contained in this book.

E-book statement: The author and publisher retain all rights to this publication. Resellers cannot place ANY limits whatsoever on this publication. Lending libraries will treat this electronic version in the same manner as the paper publication for lending purposes.

CONTENTS

Introduction	3
Where to Start	5
Doing the Chores	11
Time, Money, & Paper	17
Finding Items	33
House vs. Home	37
Decorating Your Way	37
Moving: Planning and Packing	42
Social Activities	50
Turn off the Television	50
Don't be Ruled by the Phone	51
Dressing Up or Down	52
Party Time	54
Traveling	57
A Few More Words	67
Further Readings	68
Forms	70
Budget Categories, Food List, Gift Form	
Index	77

INTRODUCTION

Your life is a messy, convoluted, mixed-up, unorganizable scream in the dark, isn't it? And if it isn't, why are you looking at this book? To gain some ideas on how to help get you organized and accomplish more? Well, read on. Perhaps I can help.

I have always been organized and many people have asked me for advice on how to organize items or a project. To them it seems I have a sense of how to organize certain items, activities, or ideas.

Take, for example, using wooden spring clothespins instead of twist ties to close bread bags and bags of snacks. It's much faster to squeeze open the clothespin than twisting open the twist tie. The clothespins will last far longer than twist ties. This is a very simple trick but I know of no one else doing this. Would you have ever thought this up?

What I'm doing in this book is sharing a lot of simple hints, ideas, tricks, suggestions, and thoughts. I've picked them up by living, reading, and talking with a whole lot of different people. I hope the suggestions given in this book improve your life and by doing so, improve the whole of humanity. I know it's too late for some of my friends, but I still love them anyway.

Your local library will have many other books on this subject and your local librarians will be happy to help you find them.

The PURPOSE OF BEING ORGANIZED is so items you need are convenient when you need them and the flow of your life is made easier.

While reading this book, I suggest you write the following sentence on a piece of paper and use it as a bookmark.

"Is there one thing I can do today that will make my life easier tomorrow?"

"So what book are you working on now, Dale?" asked my friend Chris.
"It's a self-help book on how to be organized."
"Okay, how do I get organized?"
"Well, what area do you want to get organized first?"
"Don't tell me the little things; just tell me how to get organized."

WHERE TO START?

How do you know what to do first? List what you want, put it in priority order, most important to least important, work on the most important one and ALWAYS return to it after interruptions.

How to rank items by priority. To determine what items on your 'to do' list are most important, use this method. Compare items to each other 2 at a time, and then compare those most important to each other. A and B compared, B wins; C and D compared, C wins; E and F compared, E wins; G and H compared, H wins. Now you compare B and C and decide which is more important and do the same to E and H. Then compare those 2. If C wins over H, then C is what you should work on first and H is 2nd. Compare B and E to see what items are 3rd and 4th. Then go back and compare A to D, and F to G to rank them 5th, 6th, 7th and 8th.

Below is a list of some items I had to do one weekend and how I ranked them.

Call girlfriend
Clean bathrooms
Cook supper
Food shop
Play videogames
Pay bills
Read magazines
Vacuum house
Wash dishes
Watch television

I rated the priority of the first two items, then the next two and so on. The most important went to the next column and those were ranked and so on until all items ended up in your priority order.

First ranking by importance shows vacuuming the house and cleaning the bathrooms should be done first.

call girlfriend			
	clean bathrooms		
clean bathrooms			
		clean bathrooms	
cook supper			
	food shop		
food shop			
			vacuum house
play videogames			
	play videogames		
pay bills			
		vacuum house	
read magazines			
	vacuum house		
vacuum house			
wash dishes			
	wash dishes		
watch television			

wash dishes			
	wash dishes		
food shop			
		cook supper	
cook supper			
	cook supper		
play videogames			
			cook supper
pay bills			
	read magazines		
read magazines			
		read magazines	
call girlfriend			
	watch television		
watch television			

Second ranking shows cooking supper is most important.

Paths to General Organization

You gotta wanna be organized.

If you don't write it down you won't remember it.

If you don't file it, you won't find it when you need it. If you can't find it within 30 minutes of serious searching you need a better filing system.

Divide the problem into smaller, manageable segments to make it easier to conquer. Work on 1 small problem at a time until it is done.

Set aside time to organize. Set priorities. Plan. Write down what you need and want to do this week and make a list for each day. Combine errands before you go out to save running around.

Keep a master list of everything. Break this into multiple lists
    People list: who to contact & about what.
    Home list: items to do around the house.
    Work list: projects and other items related to work.
    Food shopping list.

Sift tasks into groups:
    routine;
    urgent;
    must think about;
    work at hand;
    completed work;
    trashcan for stuff you don't have to bother with.

Put everything aside except the 'work at hand' and work on that until it is done.

I carry a small notebook in which to write my master list and break out my other lists. Each day, I write out a list of activities I want to do. There are high-priority items, somewhat important items, and necessary but could wait items. As I get them done, I cross them off. The items also take various levels of energy, so I can shift according to my energy level.

Organization folders I have at home:
- one for each bank or credit card account;
- automotive;
- medical;
- current personal items;
- stuff to mail to friends;
- music;
- travel;
- local info;
- equipment info;
- books,
- utility bills,
- house info.

Organization folders I have at work (both electronic and physical):
- company info,
- new organization info,
- department memos,
- supplies/stationary/forms,
- shipping & faxes,
- local info,
- work to write up,
- info requests,
- professional societies,
- companies I deal with,
- bills & invoices.

Keep in one folder all the information about your appliances (vacuum cleaner, TV, computer, radio, stereo, etc.). When you need a part, all the information will be easy to find. You could leave instruction manuals and warranty cards in the folder.

To change your packrat collecting habits, use these 3 steps.

1. Store items vertical to make them easier to find. You don't have to lift anything off it to see what it is. Put papers in folders in a filing cabinet or cardboard box.

2. Ask 4 questions about each item to help you decide if you need to keep it.
1) Have I used this in the last year?
2) What are the results of throwing it away?
3) What support does it give me, my office or company?
4) Can I find this information again?

3. Trash stuff. What items haven't you used in the past year that would be useful to someone else? What books could you give away to your library? What magazines could you take into work, or a doctor's or dentist's office? Look at everything in relation to your life priorities and if it doesn't support your priorities, get rid of it. Start a quarterly or semi-annually review to see what you can get rid of. If you can't decide, box it up, and look at it in 6 or 12 months.

People keep items because they remind them of what they used to be and perhaps should be (old athletic trophies, college items, military gear, toys, etc.), think they might have a use for it someday, or because an item brings back an important memory. To clean up clutter, first do small projects such as a closet, a bookcase. Sort items and place into boxes labeled 'throw away', 'give away', and 'storage'. If you haven't used an item in the past year or if there is no value to it get rid of it. Items with sentimental value should be put in a box and stored for 6 months. After that time, get rid of the box if you haven't used any of those items. Get rid of 'throw away' and 'give away' boxes within 1 week while you are in the cleaning mood.

Use small steps to organization.
    Set up a work area with the supplies you need.

Put all bills in a 'to be paid pile' and write the due date on the outside envelope. Sit down one night a week to pay bills due the next week.

Keep a bulletin board or a calendar near the phone to write down meetings and appointments.

Carry a notebook and write down ideas and to-do lists.

Make folders (checking and saving accounts, credit cards, house bills and receipts, automotive, doctors and dentists, utility bills, etc.), and throw statements, letters, etc. in the folders. Trash the envelopes unless they are registered mail or you need the return address.

Keep a book, magazine, or notebook in the car so you can use any time spent waiting.

Make a priority list each day and do the most value-added activities first.

Use a calendar with big daily squares as a catch-all file. In December or January write all the birthdays, anniversaries, and special dates on it. Keep phone numbers in the back. Write appointments down as soon as you make them. Put it close to the phone so you can write items down and check on dates. If you check your calendar at the beginning of the month and list all the birthdays, you can shop for all the birthday cards at 1 time.

Ever take some letters with you and forget to mail them? Put them up on the car dashboard so they are always in view.

DOING THE CHORES

"Chore: noun: a small or odd job; plural, the regular daily light work of a household or farm. United States use". That definition is from my Webster's New International Dictionary of the English language; Second Edition, Unabridged. Copyright 1934. My edition published in 1942.

Some people hate the word chore. It sounds too much like work. But that's exactly what chores are, the daily work of the household or farm. If you don't do the chore of bringing in wood or coal or having your oil tank filled, you will freeze. If you do not do the chores of food shopping and preparing and eating food, you will starve. If you do not do the chore of cleaning your house you will live in a pigsty. Now I've seen some nice pig sties, but it's not where I want to live.

Going Food Shopping

Never shop on an empty stomach. Your stomach will lead you into impulse buying your wallet will regret. Make a list. Stick a piece of paper on the fridge and mark down when you are low or out of something. See the food list in the back of the book and customize it to your likes and dislikes.

Every time I go to the supermarket I see people clutching little lists of things they are going to buy and on their faces are a "deer in the headlights" look of "what am I forgetting?" Hey, stupid people!! If you shop for the same things month after month, why not make a shopping list of everything you might buy and just mark that list when you need an item. I have been doing that for over 30 years and I don't consider myself too bright.

End of aisle displays are not always bargains. Compare prices. It is usually cheaper to buy ingredients and make a salad at home than to buy it from a salad bar, but consider the time saved. Buy sliced meats and cheeses instead of that deli sandwich. Buy the smallest size of a new product, if you don't like it, then you haven't wasted much money. Toiletries, shampoos, deodorants, etc., usually are less expensive at discount drug stores than supermarkets. Store bakery items are usually more expensive than items from outside. Don't take children with you, if you have a choice. They will ask, beg and whine for items they and you don't need. If you have to bring children give them coupons and have them help you find the products. Remember, the basics (milk, eggs, butter, etc.) are always far away from the entrance to make you buy something else as you walk in and out.

Write down prices of products at various stores so you can find where certain items are cheapest. Carry a calculator to figure out the price per unit for different brands or sizes of the same item. Divide price by weight or volume. Most stores put popular items at eye level to encourage impulse buying. Look at the upper and lower shelves.

Coupons save money so use them. If you find mail-in rebates, use them too. Only clip coupons for products you usually buy and items you'd like to try. Make a portable filing system by using large envelopes held together by rubber bands. Mark the envelopes with product categories (dairy, meat, frozen foods, cereals, paper products, personal items, etc.). Send in for rebates and refunds. The forms are usually on the supermarket bulletin board or in magazines. You will need some proof of purchase from the container or the store receipt.

Check out wholesalers, baked-good outlets, local farms and roadside stands. Stock up during sales if you have the room to store items. You don't have room? Look for space under your bed, couch and in your closets. Stack it in the corner and throw a colorful blanket over it. Sometimes buying in bulk saves. Check out the savings. Join with other friends to buy items and split them up. Plan meals in advance, check what ingredients you have and make your list. Check out specials in the supermarket fliers. Check out marked down items such as day old bread from the bakery, or cold cuts from the deli, or the produce section. Check unit prices on packaged items. Use pasta and rice instead of meats. It's healthy and saves money so use meat as a treat. Buy whole chickens and turkeys because the price between whole and sliced up is tremendous. Buy meat on sale and freeze it. Use leftovers. Cut the greens off vegetables, add leftover meat and cook in broth for soups or stews. Milk is cheaper in larger containers. Keep bread in the freezer and thaw slices when you need it so it won't spoil. Shop for the best buy, not by the brand name. Aspirin is aspirin. Buy plain and add extras. Buy frozen bread dough and add garlic powder or cinnamon and honey to make tasty bread cheap.

I suggest a look at Carl Japikse's "The $1.98 Cookbook: How to Eat Like a Gourmet and Save $6,000 a Year".

Make a shopping list to prevent random buying. If there is one close by, try shopping one of the many discount stores selling quality merchandise. Or perhaps a factory outlet store. Sometimes what are called big box stores have better values than smaller supermarkets but you should always compare prices. Look at the entire group of products before you decide what to buy unless you have a preference for a specific brand. Sometimes generic items can offer savings but the quality may vary. Compare the national brands and the house brands as well as the generic brands to see what may be cheaper.

Don't forget to bring along your own shopping bags to carry your groceries. I use bags that are bigger and stronger than the plastic ones the stores give out. I pack my own groceries and put all the fridge and freezer items into the same bags and the cupboard and panty items into other bags so they are easier to sort and put away when I get home.

If you plan your meals for the entire week, you will know what you need to purchase. For example I usually have pasta or spaghetti every Monday night. This is because sometimes I am tired after the first work day of the week and I want a simple easy quick meal to make, eat and clean up. When I do make something a little bit more elaborate, I usually prepare a double recipe. If I make lasagna, I make two pans of it and freeze one pan. When I make soup, I will freeze a portion in a large empty yogurt or cottage cheese container. Now I have soup to defrost and eat later. When I make meatballs or hamburgers at home I usually will make 2 or 3 pounds of ground beef into meatballs or hamburgers. Bake the meatballs on a flat tray or cookie sheet, let cool, and freeze in Ziploc bags in the freezer. The burgers are put in layers with wax paper between them and also frozen in plastic bags. This takes up less space in the freezer, and I have meatballs and burgers ready to defrost and eat any night.

You can see the food shopping list in the back of the book is arranged by categories making it easy to look for what I need as I get to that section of the supermarket and it easy to remember what to buy. I may go to the big box stores and buy large quantity of items because I have room to store them. Then I get the other items from our regular local supermarket.

I usually go shopping Tuesday or Wednesday because there are fewer people shopping. Most people, it seems, shop Thursday, Friday, Saturday or Sunday. By Tuesday the stores have restocked with fresh produce and meats and I don't have to fight the crowds.

Cleaning

You do not have to be a fanatic about cleaning. You do not have to do the dishes every day or vacuum the house every week. Unless you really want to. I often take a small brush and dustpan to walk around and sweep up piles of dust or dog fur once week or so. I vacuum the house once a month giving it a good thorough cleaning which includes moving all the furniture. I don't run the dishwasher every day. I wait till it is full of dirty dishes and then run it. I bought a new dishwasher two years ago and the manual said the normal cycle time for washing the dishes was three hours. What foolishness. When I run it now I push the "half-full" button and it runs for 1 and a half hours and it saves time, money and water. The dishes get just as clean. I never use the drying cycle of the dishwasher because it never completely dries the dishes. When the dishwasher finishes, I open the door, turn off the dishwasher and let everything air dry. Saving money again.

Another good tip for cleaning is to clean up as you're going along. If you spill something or have crumbs from a meal, wipe it up right away so you don't have a stain from the spill or the crumbs don't get scattered all over the house. Usually I wipe down the kitchen counters every day either before or after a meal so I don't get a buildup of dirt or stains which would require a lengthy cleaning. I rarely eat anywhere besides the kitchen or dining room. This way if there is a mess or spills it stays just in those parts of the house.

I have the habit of returning things to their proper place so I never have to look for something. I always know where the scissors, pliers, screwdriver, and other tools are. This saves me time when I need a tool. I also do the small chores as they need to be done instead of putting them off. It gets them out of the way and I feel better about them. For example, every day I take the recycling bin from under the kitchen sink and empty it into the recycling bins in the garage. This keeps the kitchen cleaner and does not take much time.

You should organize your day or the jobs that need to be done around the house so your housework is done either only in the morning or in the afternoon and you're not trying to do everything in one day. You could set up a routine of simple jobs to do in the evenings such as throwing a load of laundry in the washer every night. You'll get a load of wash done and you can either throw it in the dryer in the morning or right before you go to bed.

Speaking of doing laundry I am amazed at the number of people that do not let the washer fill up with water before they add the clothes. If you put the clothes in first, you will never get a full tank of water. The clothes must move freely around in the washer so every part of them is washed with water and soap. If you fill it full of clothes before filling it with water, your clothes will not be as clean.

If you throw in something that is not colorfast and all of your wash turns that color, pink, blue or whatever, remove the colored article and throw everything right back in and wash it again. You may be able to save the clothes before the color sets. And of course you know not to pour bleach directly in the water when your clothes are in the washer. Add the diluted bleach first or wait until the wash cycle has run about halfway through.

Check all the clothes labels to see what temperature you should dry them at. Most can be dried in a regular tumble dryer at low heat. Of course you know to shake the clothes out as you take them from the washer to put in the drier. I have two clothes drying racks upon which I often lay the delicate fabrics instead of throwing them in the dryer. I prefer to use thick wooden or plastic hangers instead of the narrow wire ones to hang our clothes. I've noticed the wire hangers often will leave a crease line on my dress shirts whereas wider wood or plastic ones will not. My dress suits always are hung on wide hangers so to provide support and give them space to air out. My dress pants are hung with pant hangers, the type that clip onto the bottom hem of the pants so the pants hang straight and never have a crease mark which they would get if you fold them over a hanger.

My clothes, specially my dress clothes, are hung so they have room to breathe and air may circulate around them. My five pair of black dress shoes are never worn day after day. I always give them two or three days to dry out after wearing. Oh, if you are going shopping for shoes you should shop in the afternoon or evening, not in the morning. That is because your feet swell during the day as you walk around and are slightly larger in the afternoon and evening and you want your shoes to be comfortable. If you buy shoes in the morning they may pinch as your feet expand.

My belts are hung by their buckles so they hang straight and have a chance to straighten out after I wear them. My ties are hung from tie racks and allowed to air out after I wear them. My sweaters are not squashed together in dresser drawers so I will not damage the fibers.

With a little bit of thinking about all the household "chores" which need to be done in your household, you can simplify the efforts needed to get them done.

TIME, MONEY and PAPER

Three of the biggest problem areas in many people's lives are time, money and paper. We claim we don't have the time for all the things we need or want to do in a day, the money to afford all the items we need or want, and all the paper in our lives is threatening to topple over and bury us. Sound familiar?

Paper

There are only 3 things you can do with any piece of paper. Well, 5 if you count origami and paper airplanes. You can trash it; file it, or take action with it. The key is deciding if the paper itself has value in some way for you. It could have financial value, being money, stocks, checks, land deeds, etc. It could have historical or sentimental value, being a diploma, photograph, letter, rock concert ticket, or child's drawing. If the paper doesn't have any value or you could replace it, than trash it.

You need 2 spots where you will handle paper. The first is the 'sorting area' where you decide what to do with the paper. The second area is where you do the 'action and filing'.

Let me tell you how I do it at home and at work. There is a small table near my front door where I toss all the mail as I come in. Before I look at it, I get out of my work clothes and exercise, do errands, or fix and eat supper. Then, relaxed, I look at the mail while sitting at my 'sorting area'. I pull out all the trash. Like pornography, you know trash when you see it. This goes right into the paper recycling bin. The catalogs and magazines I wish to look at go into my catalog and magazine piles. The bill and letters I open. On the bill's envelopes I write the due date and put them in a 'pay' pile. The letters I read, either trash or save in a 'answer' pile, 'file' pile or 'letters from friends' pile. That's it, mail taken care of.

Once or twice a month I sit at my desk, pay the bills, get them ready to mail out, and file the statements in folders in my desk. I have a folder for each bank and the checking and credit card statements go in there. I save the utility statements for over 1 year just in case there are any questions about them, and then I trash those statements. I can also look back at the cable or phone statements to see if I can move to a less expensive plan.

At the same time I handle the `file' pile. It may be health related letters, mutual fund statements, an article torn from a newspaper or magazine, or any paper that has value (remember financial, historical or sentimental?) to me. It could even be an invitation to a niece's or nephew's birthday party which I save and send to them on a future birthday. All of these go into folders in my file cabinet.

The folders are:
family,
financial (one each for each credit card account),
medical,
music,
travel,
local area info,
books, and equipment information (where I put operating manuals and warranty cards).

These folders will over time get a lot of papers in them so I go through them about every year and weed out what doesn't appeal to me anymore. Any papers with personal information go through a paper shredder. Remember, if you can find the information someplace else such as the library when you need it, don't keep the paper.

Once I read a magazine or catalog, I get rid of it. I copy articles I wish to keep and pass the magazine on to friends or recycle it.

At work I do the same. I handle the mail at a table, not at my desk, trashing non-value items. Then the mail gets put into folders according to priority level. `Today', `this week', `next week', and `when I get time', are the folder headings. I keep `today's' folder out on my desk so I can work on it and the other folders are set aside. When I get items done, the paperwork gets filed in folders or binders with project names on them for future reference. If information comes to me having something to do with a project, it gets stuck in that project folder.

Every night, I clean my desk so only the items I need the next morning are in front of me when I come in. `This week' and `next week' folders sit at the side of the desk and projects get moved from one to the other or into the `today' folder.

At times I scan articles into folders on my computer so I don't have to fill file cabinets with paper. Sometimes it is easier to search and find an article this way.

Time

Rules of Time Management:
    Time is your scarcest resource since you can't get it back.
    Results are more important than efforts so make sure you work on the right activities.
    Learn to say NO.
    You need uninterrupted time in which to work.
    You must be flexible yet committed in your work.

Tools for Time Management:
    ATTITUDE. It will take time to establish your habits of time organization.
    The HABIT of writing items down and carrying pencil and paper to do it.
    A portable CALENDAR with lots of space and daily and monthly pages.
    TWO LISTS: your main life goals and a to-do list of activities which will move you towards them.
    The habit of PRIORITIZING tasks. Rank them so you will work on what achieves the best results for you.
    A SYSTEM for making and keeping notes of commitments and the follow-up procedures to meet them.
    Mental relaxation periods.

Process of Time Management:
1. List your major life goals, the activities needed to get to them and break those activities into manageable steps.
2. Look how you currently use time and note any nonproductive time.
3. Block out time in advance on your calendar. Write down holidays, vacation times, annual conventions or meetings and when annual or monthly reports are due.
4. Write your to-do lists with ACTION verbs.
5. Rank and prioritize everything.
6. Break big projects into chores you can easily handle. Build some slack time into your job estimates.
7. Do the top priority items first.
8. Write it down, do it, review it. Everyday. Review what you accomplished today and plan tomorrow's work.
9. Look for uninterrupted chunks of time in which to work. Make an appointment with yourself if you need to get some free time.
10. Plan your phone calls.
11. Do your job, let others do theirs. Don't be the person everyone comes to for help.
12. Don't waste other people's time.
13. ALWAYS ask yourself 'Is what I'm doing right now the best use of my time?'

You can't use the time available to you effectively unless you manage it. Grab paper RIGHT NOW and make these lists:
    day-to-day appointment calendar,
    small notebook,
    'to do' list.

The day-to-day appointment calendar is used for writing down your upcoming chores and appointments. I use the type which shows a week at a time so I can see if I have a medical appointment, date with an intelligent attractive woman, fishing trip, party, chore such as picking up clothes from the cleaners, or phone call to make coming up. Use this calendar along with the large one by your phone to keep track of events so when you make plans with someone, it gets written immediately on both calendars. The small notebook is carried with the appointment calendar and used for keeping lists and making notes to you. For example, if you see by your appointment calendar that you have certain events in the coming week, you will make a list in your notebook.

For example, in the coming 2 weeks I have several activities to do so I write them out like this.
- In the appointment calendar:
Wed. call Jeff on Montreal trip.
Thur. call Dean to get together this weekend.
Fri. meet Liza at 7 for dinner and drinks.
Sat. fishing.
Sun. food shop, clean apt.
Tues. pack for Montreal trip.
Wed. call Kim on fishing trip and call parents.

- In the notebook I write a heading and a list under it:
-`Montreal trip': clothes, camera & film, hotel reservation letter, money, food cooler, book, rain gear, maps.
-`Dean': return his movies, photos of Civil War reenactment, beer.
-`Liza': concert tickets, blues festival.
-`fishing trip': fishing gear, waders, tackle box, clothes and rain gear, tent & sleeping bag, food coolers, camera & film, squirt guns.

See how the two work together to remind you of upcoming events and what is needed for those events? The calendar jogs your memory and the notebook fills in the details. The piece of paper called your `to-do' list is in your pocket every day. I clip my list to a pen after work so every morning when I grab that pen to put it in my shirt pocket I automatically put my `to-do' list in with it.

Let's look at my `to-do' list for this upcoming week. I made it last Friday afternoon and added a couple items over the weekend. One side of the paper has the days of the week and

what I want to do on each day, the other side has general chores listed.
- Monday: email Dean, Chris, go to gym
- Tuesday: buy birthday cards, movie?
- Wednesday: pull camping & fishing gear out
- Thursday: gym, pack for fishing trip
- Friday: load car, off fishing

The other side has these general chores that could be done on any day.
- Call parents, Kim, Liza, Jeff, Jill;
- shine shoes;
- supplies for camping: food, drinks, suntan lotion, etc.;
- do laundry;
- invite Lily and Beth over for dinner.

If someone tells me about a good book, restaurant, bar or I hear something interesting on the radio or TV, I jot it down in my notebook. I find a list usually gets filled up in two weeks so I transfer everything not done to a new list or into the back pages of my notebook. In the notebook I make lists of books, music, restaurant listings and the like, so when I go to the library, bookstore or music store I can look them up. I ask people about restaurants, read their ads in the yellow pages and look for reviews in the papers which gives me an idea of what they are like and if I should go there.

One big factor is when in the day you are most efficient. Are you a morning person or evening person? If you haven't figured that out, mentally track how you feel at different times of the day. You could keep a paper record by jotting down each hour if you are feeling tired, okay, or energetic but I think most people by their late teens or early twenties know when they feel best during the day. Once you know this, you can plan to do work best fitting your energy level.

If you are a morning person, use this time to work on projects before your workday gets busy. If you are an evening person, do work in the evening. If you can, try to work in an afternoon nap to keep energy levels high.

Practical factors will enter in how you manage time because outside factors will limit the performance of certain tasks. Store hours, doctor, dentist, or bank hours will limit when you can use their services. If many tasks are piling up, it is worthwhile to take a day off work and do those tasks. I have often wondered why a business doesn't open very early to cater to these morning people, or open late and close very late to serve evening people. If two dentists overlapped their office hours, they could open at six am and close at ten pm and serve people before or after working hours. Many successful food service businesses are only open part of the day so why don't other businesses follow this line of thinking. And why aren't services used by entire families like libraries, open on Sundays? Besides the lack of library funding of course.

Deadlines will affect your time management. I'm going on a camping/fishing trip this weekend so certain tasks have to be done before I leave Friday. Knowing this, I'll start putting items in a pile today so by Thursday night when I do my final packing, everything will be at hand and I won't be looking for anything. I won't be able to do other items this weekend so I'll write them in my notebook and plan to do them next week after I return.

We procrastination and put off unpleasant, difficult, or threatening tasks that appear complex, or time-consuming. We do it because it is a habit we've learned.

You can beat procrastination by reminding yourself of the bad results, by rewarding yourself after working on the project, and by working on small bits at a time.

Everyone procrastinates. Some of you even more than me. Here are some tricks I use to beat my tendency to procrastinate. I take small baby steps when doing a project. I didn't try to write this entire book at one time I only wrote one section, another, and then another. I only envisioned the entire book when I conceived it, and after I printed out drafts to edit it. I rewarded myself after completing each of those little baby steps. My ONLY goal for today is to edit this section on time management and after that is done I will open a bottle of wine and read. Knowing a reward is waiting and it is within reach is a good way to keep plodding along.

RESULTS BEFORE REWARDS!!

I have also mentally made a movie about this book. I see myself writing and finishing it, holding the published book in my hands, going on an author tour, being on talk shows, and talking about this book to encourage sales. Since I see this book done and myself receiving the rewards from it, it gives me the energy to keep working.

Break up your day into small segments of time. 5, 10 or 15 minutes max. It's easy to work on a task for a segment of time because you see the end of it. Start your day by finishing something. That gives you a feeling of accomplishment and it is easier to go on to the next task knowing you have something out of the way. Reward yourself after finishing a task or a job. This teaches you to focus and finish a task to get that reward.

Make your work area as comfortable and pleasant as possible so you work as efficiently as you can. If your work area has materials close at hand, if it is physically and ergonomic comfortable with good lighting and ventilation you will produce more and better work.

Concentrate your time and effort to be effective. Maintain a steady pace. Build an extra amount of time in to handle interruptions and delays. Quit when your mind starts dragging and start fresh later or the next day. Block out segments of quiet time to work on major projects. Be aware of your daily rhythms and take advantage of them. Look for new technology to help you. Set priorities and work on the most important task first. Delegate work if you can.

Time management must deal with events in your life you have some control over. Focus on what is most valuable to you. Once you have decided what is most important to you, and have written it down to carry with you, it is easy to measure any event or request against your value list.

Be flexible in your thinking and analyze possible alternatives when you plan your time. Can you do two activities at once, like read and do your laundry or drive and listen to books on tape? Must you belong to all the organizations you do? Could you drop out of one to add more time for those VERY IMPORTANT life goals you desire? Why don't you design a perfect day five years from now? List everything you do from the time you rise in the morning to the time you retire at night and list what you MUST do to obtain that perfect day. Seeing what is required for your happiness in the future may spark some thoughts about how you are spending the present.

Decide how often a household chore needs to be done. Some items need to be done everyday, like cleaning up after meals, putting away the clothes you wore, picking up the living room. Other chores might only be done twice or even once a week. Vacuuming, cleaning the bathroom, doing laundry, mowing the lawn. You may want to do certain chores at certain times. Pick up the living room just before you go to bed, or do the laundry every Saturday or Sunday morning.

Take a day off from work to do chores so you can free up your weekend. Use a day to do laundry, shopping, dishes, cleaning, pay bills or whatever usually takes time on the weekend. Get up at your usual time for an early start and to keep your weekday rhythm. I took today (a Friday) off. It is now 9:50 am and I've done laundry, dishes, shined shoes, and packed for my trip. Now I'll go food shopping, eat lunch, nap, workout, shower, and do some reading before leaving at 3. I'll come home on Sunday knowing no chores are waiting.

Money

Money Pie
Picture your income as a pie you cut up each pay period and your expenses as items that eat your pie. Chewing up your pie are your living expenses, your savings, your insurance, your or your children's education, your investments, and your retirement. Of course, before you cut the pie, the federal and state taxes take their big slice. So look at who is getting the biggest piece, where you would like to have a bigger piece, and think of ways to do so. It usually is easiest to decrease your living expenses.

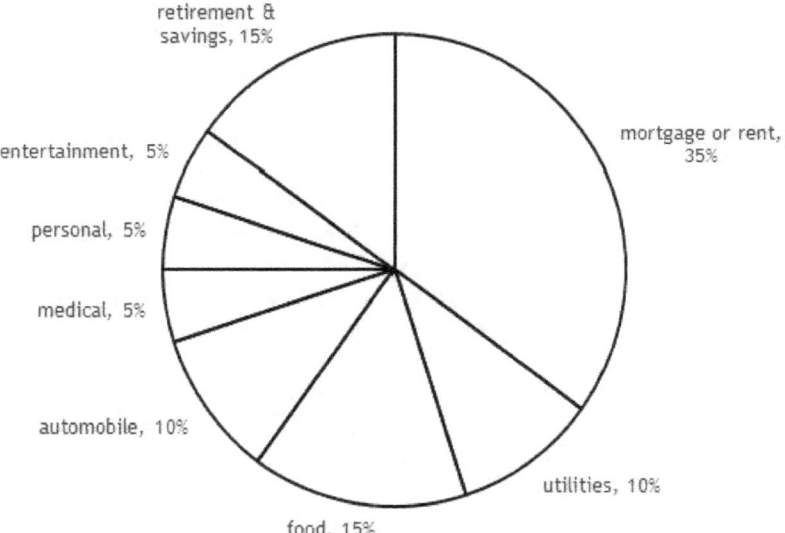

Your financial well-being depends on:
    a steady source of income;
    spending less than you make;
    the ability to cover short and long-term needs;
    beating inflation every year you can;
    paying your savings first, by automatic deductions into a savings account, mutual fund, IRA or 401(K) plan at work;
    paying off credit cards;
    saving for a real need, not a want (save for retirement, not a vacation);

doing it now.

Plan for expenses you know are coming. Utility bills, car insurance and expenses like inspections and repairs come along regularly. Put a sum aside each pay period for the bills you know are coming.

Make small changes in your life-style. Buy a car that isn't top of the line but will perform the function of transporting you safely. Then while your friends are complaining of their expensive car payments and insurance bills, you will be saving. Not living in the most exclusive neighborhood but in a good one will save money on housing. Drink bar brands instead of top shelf money. Think about your goals and your real spending. Charting out checkbook payments for the last 3 years can show where money is going and some activities you might cut back on.

Attack the big debts first. List every bill, its minimum payment per month, and what the interest rates are for each bill. Pick the bill with the highest interest rate, and pay some extra each month until it is paid. Then pay off the next highest. Paying off a credit card with an 18 to 20% finance charge will gain you more than paying off a bill with a much lower finance charge.

Retirement

Let's talk about retirement. I know, it's a long way away and you have more important items to worry about now. WRONG!! Wouldn't you retire right now to do the activities you love if you had the money? I would and so would most of the people I know. They might work at something but it would be something they love to do, not something to make a living at.

Most of us don't work the first 20 years of our lives. Most of us don't work the last 20 years of our lives either. During those 40 years we are consuming, not producing. This means we only have the time between those periods to produce the money to live on in retirement. And you know we have other expenses during the years we are working. Reviewing the rising cost of everything, including taxes, it is plain to see we can't expect our living costs to decrease when we retire. Pension plans and social security won't cover the increase in our expenses. You save today so you can have more to spend tomorrow, next week, or next year. It's that simple. If you think you can't save 10% of your income, you're overspending right now and need to review your spending patterns.

Budget

Use a budget as a planning tool to see where your money is going, and where you want it to go (your goals). It will warn you when you are spending on something that doesn't take you toward your goal.

Write down your goals at the top of the budget for inspiration. Gather and organize these financial records: paycheck stubs to see how much is coming in, tax returns, credit card bills, checkbook and bank statement to show spending.

First, identify spending by pulling out last year's bills, bank records, and checks. Divide those amounts into spending categories such as:
        rent or mortgage,
        heat and other utilities,
        phone,
        food;
        auto bills and other transportation
        repairs,
        insurance;
        clothing;
        child care;
        gifts and holiday spending;
        medical and dental;
        entertainment
        personal needs.

If you haven't saved all your spending records for a year, start now.

You have 3 types of expenses:
1. bills you must pay to live, such as rent or mortgage, and utilities,
2. bills that can be lower, such as food, auto, clothing, gifts and holiday spending,
3. expenses that could be cut such as entertainment.

Figure out what you really need and want. What gives you pleasure and value and what doesn't? If you love something like golf, sailing or concerts, then save money to do those activities. But if you only golf or sail twice a year, if the golf club membership or the sailboat worth the cost?

Credit Cards

Cut down on credit cards. Do you really need all the ones you have? Get rid of the ones charging the highest rates of interest first. Join a credit union if you can because they charge lower rates than most banks.

Destroy those pre-approved credit card applications you get. Cut the card up so someone can't send it back with a change of address and charge items to you. Call the 3 companies that keep credit ratings and ask to be taken off the pre-approved list so you will not get any pre-approved credit cards or loans. Ask at the local library or your bank for their websites or phone numbers.

Sign your new cards immediately when you get one. Don't write the credit card number on a check, just the last four digits. Don't give your number out over the phone unless you call to order something. When you charge something, make sure you get a copy of the charge statement and all carbons are destroyed. Destroy your charge statement later so no one can get your number, name and expiration date from it. If you don't get your monthly billing statement on time, call the company. Always review your statements to make sure nothing is on it that you didn't put there. Ignore credit cards with extras. Any basic card does the same thing as a gold, platinum, or special card.

If you are looking for a loan, ask questions about rates early in the negotiations. Most places don't want you to know this but there is always room to negotiate. Negotiate everything as a package: interest rates, repayment schedule, collateral, balances. Don't postpone the discussion of rates. This may put you under the pressure of facing a deadline.

Shopping

Always shop with a list no matter what you are shopping for. When shopping for a major item, ask why you need this item, what features you need, what your budget is, and what features would be extras. Do your research by reading Consumer Reports, other magazines and websites, and asking friends. Don't stick with brand loyalty. Take along a digital camera so you will have pictures of choices to think over later. Take notes in the store about the different types, features and prices. Ask if they have catalogs with information about the item. Ask how one brand compares to another in price, value, longevity, features, etc. Ask about the store's service and delivery policy. Don't be impressed with new technology, it adds to the cost, and can be costly if the features break. Do you really need electronic touchpads on your toaster? Read the warranties and guarantees. Don't buy service contracts. The manufacture's warranty is usually good enough. Take your time, and give yourself a day or three to think about what will suit your needs.

Annual sale times (Check Consumer Reports for the details of this list):
  January - after Christmas and New Year sales are linens (white sales), appliances, men's suits, and furniture.
  February - china, glass, silver, mattresses, bedding.
  March - ski equipment, pre-season spring clothing sales.
  April - clothing, especially after Easter.
  May - carpets, rugs, household cleaning products.
  June - furniture.

July - sports equipment, sportswear, gardening supplies and tools.

August - any summer item is marked down. Yard tools, camping equipment, lawn movers, outside furniture, barbecues. Also good buys on cars.

September - buy school clothes at the end of the month.

October - the early sales for the holiday season start.

November - women' coats, men's suits, most everything woolen.

December - cars.

General Savings Tips
If you aren't carrying the cash you are less likely to spend it.
Toss pocket change into a container. It adds up fast.
Don't have a lot of savings and checking accounts or credit cards because service fees add up fast. Start saving habits as soon as possible. No matter how little it is money adds up fast.

Jog in the street or a park. Buy weights and use at home. Why pay health club costs if you can do it elsewhere? Eating out is cheaper at lunch than dinner. Take advantage of buffets at 'happy hours' but eat the healthy stuff, not the salty, fatty items. Go to movies when they offer discount rates. I usually go Monday nights because there are fewer people. Buy clothing that doesn't need dry cleaning. Shop at thrift stores, yard sales, auctions, and flea markets. Borrow items you use occasionally and return them promptly in good condition. Swap magazines with friends. Sell items you don't use anymore.

Turn off the lights when you leave a room. Save supermarket plastic bags for garbage bags. Reuse everything you can. Buy after holidays. Christmas decorations right after Christmas or the New Year. Buy reusable items, such as cloth napkins, handkerchiefs, and cloth diapers instead of disposable ones.

Replace incandescent bulbs with fluorescent bulbs to save money. Unplug electrical items that have 'instant on' features when you go away on trips. They use electricity all the time. I plug all my electronics into surge suppressors and turn off everything with one switch when I am not using them. Put a small plastic jar or jug filled with water or small stones in the toilet tank to reduce the amount of water used when flushing. In summer, open windows to let in cool night air and close them in the morning to keep your house cool in the day. Use ceiling fans in summer to cool the room and in winter to force warm air down from the ceiling. Leave south facing window curtains and blinds open during sunny winter days to gain solar heat and cut down on heating bills. Seal all windows and doors to reduce air leaks. Even thin pieces of cardboard placed between window frames help slow air loss. If you have an air conditioner or kitchen fan, remove the inside cover and put in plastic to cover the opening and stop drafts. Remove in spring. Wear a sweater or hat and lower heat by 2 to 4 degrees.

Drink water instead of soft drinks. It's better for you and much cheaper. Keep a bottle or jug of water in the fridge to drink from instead of running the tap each time you want a drink.

Hanging on the wall above my writing desk is a piece of paper with three questions on it which helps me focus on what is important to me.

WHERE DO YOU WANT TO BE?

WHAT DO YOU WANT TO BE DOING?

WHAT ARE YOU DOING TO GET THERE?

FINDING ITEMS

Sometimes you need to find something and you have no idea where to start, much less the entire process you have to go through. Some items are easy. A phone number? Where you can buy something? Look in the phone book. But sometimes items aren't so simple. Many items are not listed in phone books. There are several people where I work that are 'professional shoppers'. When I need to find something, I ask them where I should go. I might have to listen to a 15 minute talk on why one store is better than another and what the best brand is and what features I should get, but it is worth it. Certain people are interested in certain activities and you go to them for help. Ask around in your workplace. You'll find some 'professional shoppers'.

Use Your Library
Check out your public library. Yes, it is YOUR public library because your tax dollars support it, just like the fire, police and public works departments. If you have not been in a library in a while it may be intimidating. Ask your friendly local librarian for help.

Be Prepared
How do you find new ideas? Carry a pen and paper or a little tape recorder. Ideas come at all times and places and you MUST write them down immediately before they escape. I carry a tape recorder with me in the car so I don't have to write while driving. Also keep paper and pencil in every room you live in, at your desk at work and in your car. I always carry a pen and paper in every jacket I wear. This is an easy habit to start and will quickly repay itself if you write things down.

Work on more than 1 project at a time. You will spark an idea at one place that could be used at another. The cross-fertilization of information, scenes, expressions, etc., will help bring out ideas. List projects and subjects you are working on and post it where you will see it often. Write an attention grabbing title for your project and post it above your work area for stimulation.

Keep your memory crisp by exercising it. Learn new skills or habits. Write out your life story. The exercise of thinking of long ago events will keep you sharp. Keeping a log of memory lapses (forgetting to turn off lights, forgetting a name or phone number, forgetting to pay something, etc.) for a month or two will show you what you need to work on.

Memory is association. Make connections between items. Memory is attention. You remember items you deliberately focus on. Memory is organization. If you always put something in the same place, you will remember where it is. Memory is imagination. If you imagine, step by step, doing something or imagine something being unusual, you remember it easier.

Why subscribe to newspapers unless have time to read them? Pick up only the weekend papers and you can stay well informed while saving money. They usually have a week in review section. Wednesday's and Thursday's papers usually have shopping ads and Friday's the weekend events. About the only thing I miss by not getting the daily paper are the comics.

When reading a newspaper, write on the first page any section and page number (B-6, for example) of an article you want to save. Before recycling the papers, check the first page for articles to save.

When you are subscribing to magazines, use as your middle initial something that will remind you of that magazine. 'B' for 'Bicycling', 'T' for 'Time', 'N' or 'G' for 'National Geographic'. This way you can track who rents, sells or gives away your name to other mailing lists and tell them to stop.

Instead of keeping a book, an article, or piece of paper with something of interest, copy the pertinent info on 1 piece of paper. Copy the title and copyright pages of a book, or the title and author and what magazine the article was in, or the address of the person or company. File these pages into a 3-ring binder, or enter in a computer database program with some keywords which will help you find it again. Or scan or photocopy the article or book title page and put in a folder marked with a phrase. I have a big, fat folder marked 'house/home' to store ideas for my dream house, another folder marked 'cartoons' where I put cartoons I like, and other folders (books, music, computer, travel, food & wine, etc.) for other subjects.

Write It Down

Write down quotes people say. I've got some great laughs, good truths and ideas this way. Other people bring different outlooks, backgrounds and experiences to blend with yours. Read everything with a quest for ideas. Does your morning paper carry an article that sparks a 'what if' in your brain? Can you put a thought from one article together with one from another to make something new? When I read newspapers and see an article I want to keep or get information out of, I write that page number on the top of the front page (A1 or NJ-12) or I bend over the pages of magazines to mark good articles and cut them out before recycling.

When I read books, I use a piece of paper for a bookmark and write down page numbers and bits of info or sayings I might want to recall later. I leave it in the book on my shelf and it helps me find things fast. If it is a library book or one borrowed, I make memory joggers in a notebook used specifically for remembering books.

Use Other's Viewpoints

Think about your friends and the work they are in. What would each of them bring to the project you are working on? Teachers, construction workers, nurses, engineers, lighting designers, firefighters, salesmen, MBA's, auto mechanics, photographers, all would approach a project with ideas different from yours. I often ask my friends who work in different professions their opinions and thoughts about the projects I work on.

Open a dictionary and skim it. Try to fit the word you see with your idea or project. Say you are trying to come up with a new decorating idea and you find the word 'tracery'. That brings to mind interlacing lines or branching lines. Could you paint over a piece of lace for a lacy effect or lightly brush on a branching effect with a different color or cover up the top 6 or 12 inches of the wall with wallpaper suggesting Gothic artwork?

I have framed some of the lace pieces my grandmother and mother made to make very unique wall decorations. Some other pieces of lace are used for summer window curtains in my kitchen. Every time I look at them they give me good memories.

Sit down with a blank sheet of paper and start writing. Something will come. If not, get up and wander around. The change of view usually helps. I often get ideas while traveling and carrying a tape recorder or notebook helps me remember them.

Read or skim magazines you don't usually look at. Read magazines aimed at the opposite sex, look at magazines aimed at businesses different from the one you're in, or magazines about a sport or hobby you don't care or know much about.

HOUSE VERSUS HOME

Decorating Styles

Your personal style should show wherever you live. The difference between a 'house' as just a place where you live and a 'home' as a place providing a congenial environment is very important. My place is decorated so people feel relaxed and informal. I want people to feel okay to take off their shoes, to raid my fridge, and to put on music they like when they visit. Far too many houses I've visited have an air about them that makes you ask permission to do anything. That's not comfortable.

A comfortable chair, good light for reading, and a flat surface within easy reach to put items on is beyond price, at least for me. What do you need to be comfortable while doing your favorite activity?

When people at work mention they are going to have a garage or yard sale, or you see a sign for one on the bulletin board, go. You learn more about that person and their lifestyle and you might pick up some good bargains. After her mother passed away, a woman at work was cleaning out her mother's house before selling it. I picked up a lot of items and she gave me a good discount off the prices.

Buying area rugs may be a better choice than wall-to-wall carpeting if you plan to move in the future. Be flexible in furniture choices. Be eclectic in decorating. It gives you a more personal and unique look. Some libraries and art galleries rent out paintings, prints, and sculpture. Check out what they have.

Maps make colorful posters and you get them with your subscription to National Geographic. I once decorated an entire hallway, including the ceiling, with National Geographic maps. That was a conversational starter. Find and shop at the outlet stores and thrift shops in good neighborhoods for high quality used furniture at low prices. Check out garage sales for items you need.

   Collect and display what you like, whatever it is. Ask what your company does with old furniture. Will it let employees take items being thrown out? Ask your friends to check where they work. While I was working at one company they were replacing their wood furniture with modular metal cubicles. I asked a friend in maintenance what they were doing with the old wood desks and he said they were putting them out for scrap. Thinking quickly, I asked for a scrap pass for two desks. Then I went to see my friend Dean who had a pickup truck. We both got a desk and a swivel chair.

   If a friend moves and is leaving something behind or trashing something, ask for it. For helping a female friend move, I got a china cabinet, a liquor cabinet, 2 end tables, and a kitchen table she didn't want. Trade skills. I helped paint a friend's apartment and refinished some of her furniture and she made me an afghan.

   Desks can be made from a door (take 1 off your closet) or a piece of plywood placed on top of 2 drawer file cabinets or milk crates. The 'college dorm' decorating style helps many people get thru years of low income. Drive around good neighborhoods the evening before garbage pickup day. Many people put out items you might use. Check out the Craigslist website for items people are giving away.

   Plants are a pleasant touch to a house or apartment. They add oxygen while cleaning the air, which helps a lot during the winter when windows are closed. Ask friends for clippings and how to take care of them.

   To store rolls of tape, unwind the neck of a wire coat hanger, slip the rolls on it, and wind the neck back together. All of your different tapes are in one place and easily found. Thanks Dad for this tip.

Collect quotes and comics or cartoons to make a collage to cover an old table or hang on a wall.

Everyone needs a set of tools. You can do many repairs with a pair of pliers, hammer, and screwdrivers of various sizes, scissors, masking and electrical tape a sturdy knife, measuring tape, nails and screws of various sizes. Ask a handy friend to help you put this collection together and show you how to do repairs. Do something for them in return.

If you use a battery charger and rechargeable batteries, it will pay for itself within 2 years, if not sooner. Check and change all batteries in your house at the same time so you know if they are good or not. List items that use batteries, smoke detectors, flashlights, cameras, computers, etc. and tape it to your charger. If you change your batteries on an easily remember date, such as your birthday or when daylight savings time changes, it is much easier to remember to do it.

Start a Home

While you are waiting for when you have enough income to decorate the way you would like to, start a file folder called 'Home'. As you come across articles or pictures that show a living space you like, stick it in the folder. If you go somewhere and see something that really strikes you, write a little note about it for the folder. Take a picture of friend's rooms if you see something you like. Does a friend have a wonderful chair you plop into every time you are in their house? Write down all the information you can find on the chair tag so you can get yourself one someday. Browse the local library's shelves in the home decorating section. Plan for the day when you can make your house a home.

Little Touches

While you are waiting to own your own house, put up little touches. Buy posters you like and have them matted and framed for your walls. Tell your artistic friends you like their work and they may give you something. Make decorations yourself. Hang up sheets of colorful fabric or towels to brighten your walls. They also help cut down on noise. Set out your collectibles, whatever they may be. If you like them enough to collect them, they are good enough to put on display. One of my friends made a collage using photos of his friends and family and mounted it in an old picture frame. He now has a colorful record of events and friends that is a conversation piece. Get your favorite photos enlarged and mounted to remind you of good times, places and friends.

Little touches of luxuries can add a lot to where you live. Cloth napkins instead of paper, classy pillows on your couch and chairs, lots of your favorite books and music, candles, pictures, lace hung over your lamps. Look at your friend's houses or apartments or through home decorating magazine for ideas.

4 Living Areas

There are only four essential areas you need, all the other are extras. You need a bathroom, a place to sleep, a place to prepare and eat food, and a living area. These areas can overlap. Each area is determined by your needs, desires and habits.

Sometimes rooms get disorganized because too many activities are being done in that room. A living room may also be used as a home office, exercise area, eating area, hobby area, napping area, television watching area, and entertainment area. These may interfere with each other. Decide which activities belong there, which don't, and shift those that don't belong, along with their clutter, into another area.

Create areas in your living space for certain activities. It is far easier to do a chore, like paying bills or writing checks, if you always do it at a certain desk or table. If you don't have the space to set aside, then create a folder to hold all items you need to do that chore. Pull the folder out, do the chore, replace everything in the folder until next time.

My friend Pete hung a 3 basket wire hanger over his bathtub. He puts his shampoo and conditioner bottles, sponges, and the like in it so he easily can reach them and they don't leave messy soap rings on the tub.

Stocking the bathroom medicine cabinet:
- first aid items: gauze pads and bandages, surgical tape, cotton swabs and cotton balls, scissors, tweezers, adhesive bandages of various sizes, hydrogen peroxide, antibiotic cream for minor cuts.
- pain, fever, and anti-inflammatory medicines: aspirin & ibuprofen. acetaminophen works on pain and fever but does not reduce swelling. Check medicines for their ingredients.
- skin protection: hydrocortisone cream for rashes, petroleum jelly for dry skin.
- poison protection: something to induce vomiting like syrup of ipecac but call emergency for help before doing so.
- instant ice and instant heat compresses.
- anything else that works for you but don't rely too much on any medicine. Cold medicines have side effects you should be aware of.

I love to cook and to me, these are vital kitchen appliances:
-microwave: nuke everything
-rice cooker: cook up a batch of rice and microwave what I need during the week
-crock pot: throw items in, turn it on, go away and come back to stew, chili, soup, etc.
-food processor: sometimes I need faster hands to chop, slice or dice large amounts
-mixer: sure beats (pun intended) my standing around hand mixing
-blender: puree, frappe, liquefy.

I was thinking about discussing ways to make food preparation much easier but since there are so many good books already written on this subject, you should go to the library and find them.

Take 15 minutes each day to do small chores around the house, like hanging up clothes, returning items to where they belong, putting books or magazines into a pile, etc. This small bit of time adds up quick and shows results.

Looking For A Place

Searching for an apartment or a house? If you're moving locally, you can ask friends where the good neighborhoods are. What's nice? Well, decide what's important to you? Being close to work, close to shopping, a quiet, safe neighborhood, close to a park, close to other friends. Weigh the options. If you're moving to another city, you can ask people you work with. Maybe your company human relations department can offer suggestions. It might be a trade off between living close and paying more and driving a bit further and paying less. You could also ask the library for information, such as crime rates, income levels, age levels, ethnic makeup and so on. Make sure you drive around in that neighborhood during rush hour. What looks like a quiet street on a weekend could turn into a turnpike when people are going to or coming from work.

Visit the local police department and ask about crime statistics (burglaries, auto theft, disturbances of the peace, etc.), in the neighborhoods or housing complexes you are looking at.

When you are looking at apartments, poke around in everything. Open cabinets, open closet doors, look under the sink. Look for evidence of water leaks, sniff for odors, and check the stove for cleanliness and gas leaks. Click all the lights on and off. Count the outlets. Are there enough? Where is the fuze box? If the landlord says they will do something or fix something, get it in writing before you sign anything.

If you rent, get renter's insurance because your landlord's insurance usually won't cover losses from fire, theft or damages.

You could ask your landlord if they would consider lowering the rent if you do repairs, yard work, or paint the place.

When looking I always write up lists of "must haves", "do not want" and "don't care" requirements. This made the search a lot easier and faster.

How to Move

I have lived in 27 different places in 7 different states so I know a little bit about moving. MAKE A LIST! Or several lists. You will need friends to help you move, unless you are lucky enough to be having a moving company do it for you. Oh, sometimes moving companies will have helpful moving lists on their websites. You will need vehicles to move items. You need to decide what you can pack away and live without for a couple weeks before and after the move.

Give yourself plenty of time to pack, 2 weeks to a month should be enough, depending on how much stuff you have. Don't move items you don't need. Have a garage sale or give them away. Don't pack items you need, such as clothes, medicine, important papers, bathroom items, etc. Don't pack valuables or specially loved items for the movers. Move them with you so you know they are safe. Have the utilities turned off after you move, not on moving day because you will still need them. Label all boxes with the room it goes into. Don't try to do a long-distance move all at once. Take your time, make it a mini-vacation, and keep track of expenses and mileage for your tax records. A mid-week is usually cheaper than a weekend move if you are renting a truck or having a company move you. Take your phone book with you to get numbers when you want to call friends or businesses back where you used to live.

Packing

Start saving newspapers, boxes with flaps or lids, and large paper bags (the size you get at the grocery store). Why? You will wrap breakables in newspapers, place with more wadded up newspapers in the boxes, tape them shut, and write what room they belong in on the outside of the box.

You can put your books in double paper bags and turn another bag upside down and slide it over the top for a lid. Makes them easier to carry than a box full of books.

Paper for copier machines comes in heavy-duty boxes with fitted lids that are wonderful for moving and storing items. Pack away winter or summer clothes, mementos, blankets, or anything else in them. The boxes are sturdy, stackable, and easy to label. They are usually free for the asking at work.

First, pack everything you aren't now using. All your books, seasonal clothing, toys, pictures off the walls, extra kitchen items. Leave out tools, some music to play and enough kitchen items to fix and eat meals with. It's easiest to pack room by room. If you pack up everything in your living room in boxes and mark them 'living room', and stack them in a corner, you can see what is left. Take apart any furniture you can and stack it against the wall. Clothes may be packed in clothes bags or in double garbage bags. Couch cushions may also be packed in heavy garbage bags to protect them. It is easiest to pack up the living room first, then any extra bedroom items, then all the kitchen stuff (leaving enough items to cook and eat with). Then the day of the move, you just have to pack a few items in the kitchen, bedroom, and bathroom.

Assign every room in your new place a color and number and mark the boxes that are going in that room with that color. Draw a map showing the rooms, the colors and the numbers and stick it by the front door. Also somehow mark each room with its color and number. Then everyone helping you can easily put items in the correct room.

Mark a couple boxes marked 'important' and throw in items you will need right after moving, like extension cords, your tools, tape, light bulbs, phone and phone books, last minute bills and mail, etc. While packing and unpacking, it is a good idea to review all your possessions and ask yourself 'Do I really need or want this?'

Planning Your Move

2 months before the move:
- get a notebook to record items in
- fill out all forms the moving company requires and if your company is paying for the move, those forms also
- collect medical and dental records, children's school records, etc.;
- have your doctor write out all your prescriptions and get them filled before you go
- close out local charge accounts at businesses
- talk to your bank about transferring your accounts to your new bank
- get letters of reference from bank, businesses, doctor, lawyer, utilities, etc. to show to businesses in new location
- go to the post office and get change of address cards and send them out to friends, magazine subscriptions, businesses, etc.
- contact insurance company to transfer all insurance
- tell local utilities to turn off service after you leave and contact utilities in new location to arrange for service to be on when you arrive
- inventory your home for insurance purposes by videotaping each item and saying what you paid for it and where you bought it
- sketch out a floor plan of your new digs and plan where your furniture will go
- start packing items you won't need
- remove everything from the walls and windows and pack it up

1 month before the move
- change address at post office and have mail forwarded
- list items you will carry with you in the car
- clean the house
- have rugs and furniture cleaned
- give away or trash everything you aren't taking
- return all items you've borrowed

- make sure your car is in good shape to make the trip
- party with all your friends

   1 or 2 weeks before the move
- pack your suitcases with clothes and personal items you will need during the move
- set out boxes for the items you will need right after you arrive and start throwing those items in there:
    > cleaning supplies,
    > bathroom & bedroom supplies,
    > first aid items,
    > medicines,
    > light bulbs,
    > tools,
    > clock,
    > radio,
    > coffee or tea and a coffee pot and cups,
- pack up the valuables you are taking with you
- eat the frozen food in your freezer
- finish your inventory, if you haven't already
- close out bank accounts
- organize items, if possible, by the rooms they will end in.

   1 or 2 days before the move
- defrost and clean the fridge, you'll be too busy to cook from now on and you won't feel like it either
- wash up all your dishes and put them away
- make sure your friends have your new address
- if a moving company is doing your packing, they usually show up on this day so work with them to ensure everything is packed up and they know where items are going in your new place.

   Moving out day
- strip your bed linens and pack them up
- double check the address on all paperwork and make sure the movers have a phone number where you can be reached
- walk through your house before the movers leave to make sure they got everything
- don't forget the garage

- give the movers a copy of the floor plan of your new digs with the furniture layout
- pack your car with everything that is going with you
- don't forget to pack the phone book
- walk through the house again to double and triple check everything is out of there
- turn off everything, lock it up and say good-bye.

Moving in day
- carry everything in from your car and put it where it belongs
- pull out your box of supplies and set it where you can get at it
- check to see that all the utilities are working. If not, call up the utility company to ask why. If no phone, go ask to use a neighbor's
- oversee the movers as they carry in your items and check off items on the inventory list
- walk through the moving van before it leaves to make sure you have everything (I lost a new broom because I didn't do this)
- some movers will unpack boxes for you and place items where you want them, this is when your floor plan comes in handy
- after they leave, relax for a while and wander around your new place
- you do not have to unpack everything on the first day or even in the first month, take your time to get accustomed to your new digs
- pick an area to place unwanted packing supplies as you empty boxes
- pick an area to place boxes that do not have to be unpacked right away making sure it is not near those packing supplies you are going to throw away.

First week or 2 in your new place
- write tips down in the notebook on how to have a better move next time
- put numbers by your phone of the utility companies, police, fire, closest hospital, the new neighbors you have met, etc.
- put your old phone book by your phone
- place ALL moving related expenses in a large envelope because you may be able to deduct them on your taxes

If I Was Organized, I'd Be A Librarian   49

- open bank accounts if you have not already done so
- go to the post office and get change of address cards and send them out to friends, magazine subscriptions, businesses, etc. if you have not done this
- check how soon you have to change your driver's license and car registration
- check with your insurance company to make sure all changes went through
- change any legal documents that may need it, like wills
- request refunds from your former utility companies, if you have not already done so
- visit the local library and get a library card. Ask for local info
- contact the local chamber of commerce for local info.

Your first month or 2
- buy two county maps. Keep one in your car. As you locate places, mark them on the map.
- ask the neighbors or people you work with where you can find good local services:
        laundromat & drycleaners & tailors,
        barber or hairdresser,
        lawyer,
        dentists, doctors & other health care,
        gas station & auto repair,
        grocery store,
        shopping centers,
        bakery,
        butcher,
        liquor store,
        drug store/pharmacy,
        appliance store,
        hardware store,
        clothing stores,
        library,
        airport & bus routes & schedules,
        city hall, police station, parks & recreation areas (may be on map),
        good radio & TV stations & cable service.

Stock your kitchen
- examine the place and list what needs to be done in the way of repairing, painting, decorating, storage areas, (both inside and outside), etc. and note how important each item is and if it needs to be done right away or can wait awhile.
- install any mechanical, electrical or safety items as soon as possible
- have a small informal house warming party inviting your neighbors. You'll learn a lot about former tenants or owners and about your new neighborhood
- get back into your old routines as soon as possible. This helps you cope with the move.
- explore your new location. Find activities you like to participate in and get involved
- invite your friends to visit your new place, even if it is a mess.

SOCIAL ACTIVITIES

You must take control over your social activities in order to maximize the benefit you receive from them and minimize the cost and time to you. What value do you receive from going out drinking four nights a week? Or spending every evening watching television, playing video games or surfing the World Wide Web?

Turn Off the Television

Plan your TV watching. Go thru the listings for the coming week and circle what you REALLY want to watch. Each night, turn the TV on for that show ONLY, then turn it off. Do other worthwhile activities instead. Don't watch TV during meals with friends or family. Use that time together to concentrate on each other. What gets the most airplay on the news? Items that are the most visually interesting, the disaster, war, fire, storm, tragedy, which are often not the most important story. Look at the book "The Psychology of Television" by John Condry.

If you have friends over, or you go to their place, don't spend the evening staring at the TV, unless that was what the plan was. Television lessens communication and invites passive activities. If you are going to watch a movie, or a sports event or a certain show, turn the TV off right after it finishes and talk about what you watched. How did what you watched relate to the real world? Did it promote the view that power or violence makes right or all problems, no matter how big, are solved in 1/2 or 1 hour? What did the commercials promote, food, alcohol, consumption of mass quantities? Did it really relax you or did it make you want to imitate what you saw on the screen? Ask yourself and your friends if they really need to watch all the shows they do? Wouldn't it be better to spend some evenings with each other playing games, cards, listening to music and just talking to each other?

The television listing comes with the Sunday newspaper and I take 10 or 15 minutes to look at the listings for the week. I circle what I REALLY want to watch, not what might be fun to watch. Then each evening after my chores like exercising, supper, doing the dishes, writing bills, etc., are done, I look at the television listings. If nothing is circled, the television **never** comes on. I find something else to do. There are always calls to make to good friends, letters to write, books to read, music to listen to, and of course, another book to write.

Don't Let the Phone Use You

We all know people who can't let a phone ring. They have to answer and see who is calling. What low self-control. Telephones, like televisions and many other machines, are a device for our use, not something which rules us. Get an answering machine and let it take your calls instead of interrupting your concentration or whatever you are doing. This will cut out a lot of telemarketers. You can also have fun thinking up creative messages to put on your machine and leave on others answering machines.

When someone calls asking for money, say "I don't give my money away." and hang up. That's all the answer they need. Phone call you don't want? Tell them good-bye and hang up.

Phone call you can't take right now? Tell them you can't talk at that moment, ask for their phone number, and call them back. Return all calls at the same time and have the information you need in front of you to answer questions.

Figure out your calling patterns to save money. Review your phone bills once a year to see:
    1. if your calls are local or long-distance,
    2. what time of day you do your calling,
    3. if you make many little calls or a few long calls.
Call up the phone companies in your area, give them this information and have them send you, in writing, the single best plan for you. Compare the plans and use the best. I recently changed my phone company and am saving over $50 a month

with the new plan. Use the phone book to look up local numbers and save directory assistance charges.

Keep a calculator near the phone so when someone calls saying they are going to send you something and all you have to do is pay a little for shipping, do the math. "You say 4 magazines for just $2.90 a week shipping. That's $150.80 a year, which works out to $37.70 per magazine." You can get most magazines a lot cheaper than that and a lot of them are free at the library.

I use a 3" x 5" card file box for people's addresses. I write an address on a card, file it and keep the box by the phone. This is easy to refer to when calling someone or when someone asks for an address and phone number. It is very easy to add changes when they move or change phone numbers and unlike an address book, you never run out of space. Just make a new card.

Keep a list of subjects you want to talk about with your far away friends. It's easy to forget items you want to ask and a list will help prevent pauses in the conversation.

Write a letter instead of phoning. It is pleasant to do and you can go into greater detail on more subjects for less money.

Dressing Up Or Down

What is your style of dress? It will directly affect social activities and your relationships. At work, when someone wears a dress shirt and a tie with jeans and sneakers, the message he is sending is he doesn't know if work is formal or informal. One friend pointed out in the engineering community you can tell when someone graduated from college because they bought a suit to look for work and they will wear that suit for many years. And the old retired men walking around wearing shorts, dark socks and dress shoes or sandals really get my fashion awards.

You don't have to stay up with the latest fashions to look good. Just pick a style and look you are comfortable with, that sends the message you want sent, and stick with it. I'm a barefoot farm boy so my style tends towards no shoes, jeans, shorts or cutoffs, and t-shirts or flannel shirts. But as a professional in the workplace I have plenty of dress clothes. When I go shopping for clothes, I buy very good quality because I know it will repay me by the length of service I get out of it.

Simplify your clothing choices. Buy good quality so it will last longer and look better. Buy conservative, traditional styles and accent them with flair. They will still be in style for four or five years. I wear only black socks and black dress shoes knowing they will match any of my blue or gray suits. Most of my dress shirts are either white or pale blue to match my suits. I spice up the look with colorful, fashionable ties. This saves me time and reduces stress.

Notice how the people above you in the organization dress and follow their lead. Polish your shoes. If people notice you don't care about your shoes, they assume you don't care about other items. One of the nicest relationships I ever had was partly because the lady noticed I was wearing high quality polished shoes. Get them re-soled and re-heeled when needed to last longer and save you money. Ask friends of the opposite sex to give you hints about your wardrobe. People will judge your economic, educational, social, moral, and success levels by what you wear. Dress so they judge you favorably. If you choose and lay out clothes the night before, it will save you time in the morning.

When I buy clothes, I will buy two or three different brands of the same item and write the purchase date inside of the collar or waist band. Then I can tell which brand wears the best over the next few years. I do this with shoes and boots too.

Social Events

At this point in your life you know what you like to do but please be willing to try new activities. Give them 1 or 2 chances, and if you don't like them, at least you can say you tried and provide reasons for not liking it. Sometimes you may do something because your friends go. I go fishing every year with friends and one of them is not interested in fishing but he comes so he can be with us. He finds other activities while we fish. I'm not too interested in car or motorcycle racing but I go to be with my friends that do. Being with them is more important to me than being at the race. It's a good time to catch up on what we are all doing and share some silliness.

Having a Party

Having a party? Good idea. Invite me. Leave something undone and ask the first guest or 2 to help you with it. This gets them involved right away and removes any awkward feelings on their part. It might be a chore like putting out glasses or napkins or something, helping set out food or putting on music.

Invite as many people as your place can hold and your party money will allow. Invite a wide mix of people from your job and social life. You met someone interesting at the Laundromat? Invite them along. If you think your doctor, dentist, or car mechanic is fun and interesting to talk to, invite them over. Make sure you invite couples (married or not) and singles.

Make the invitations 2 or 3 weeks ahead to give people time to plan for it. Draw up little maps for those who don't know how to get to your place. Maps are easier than giving verbal directions. Saturday night is a good time for a party because it gives you a day to prepare, a day to clean up and no one has to worry about working the next day.

If I am not doing a sit-down dinner party, I set out a food buffet. Skip the little appetizers and set out foods in bulk like chili, potato or pasta salads, cheese platters, rolls, sliced ham or turkey, pastas, rice, pizza, and vegetables. Cook food ahead of time if you can, like the ham or turkey, rice and pasta. The day of the party you can cook up the last minute items, pick up the ice, do the last minute housekeeping, set up the bar, take a relaxing bath or shower, set up the bathroom, fill the coffee urn and set out the food dishes.

Use disposable plastic plates, glasses, and utensils and paper napkins. Use your mixing bowls, cutting boards, regular dinner plates and the like as serving dishes. Set the food buffet away from the bar and put them out of heavy traffic areas like doors and the bathroom. Get plenty of ice cubes, 2 or 3 times what you think you will need. You don't want to run out. If you have an extra plastic wastebasket, line it with a garbage bag and put the bags of ice cubes in there. They will keep cold and be handy for the bar.

Serve coffee. If you don't have a large coffee maker, ask friends if they have one you could borrow. You don't want to keep running into the kitchen to make up 6 cups of coffee in your little coffee maker. Or pour the coffee into a thermos bottle and start another pot right away. On weekends I make a full pot of coffee, pour it into my thermos so I can have coffee anytime I want.

Bar

What should you have at the bar? Depends on the crowd, their tastes, the season and what is currently in fashion, but here is a list of suggested items that will cover most tastes.

Must haves:
    beer,
    red and white wine,
    hard liquor (vodka, gin, scotch, rum, bourbon, etc.)
    mixers (cola, club soda, tonic water, ginger ale, orange juice, grapefruit juice, tomato juice, lime juice)
    lemons and limes for garnishes.

Good extras:
    Liquors (sweet vermouth, tequila, sherry, Campari, triple sec)

Garnishes (olives, little pearl onions, maraschino cherries, salt and pepper, Tabasco and Worcestershire sauce.)

Stocking Your Bar

A bottle or two from the six most popular liquor types; gin, vodka, whiskey, scotch, bourbon, rum and perhaps a bottle of tequila. Also beer (both domestic and imported), red and white wine and some liqueurs and brandy. What brands to buy? Ask your friends what they like and buy that. Or just try a lot of everything and make up your own mind.

You will also need mixers: bottled spring water, cola and diet cola, ginger ale, tonic water, club soda, orange, tomato, and grapefruit juices. You will use these as alternatives for alcohol so have plenty on hand for the party. Sometimes tap water can give an off taste to a drink so use bottled spring water. For garnishes you might need oranges, lemons, limes and olives.

Buy a good book on mixing drinks and refer to it. Also buy a good corkscrew for the wine and a jigger to measure with and a shaker set with a strainer. Don't forget something to keep your ice in.

What glasses to serve drinks in? I say anything that will hold the liquor is fine but some stuffy types like classy glasses. Glasses are often on sale so shop around. You'll need both short (6 oz.) and tall (10 oz.) straight-sided glasses for the tonic and soda drinks, highballs, and spring water drinks. Your drink book will tell you what drinks go in what glass.

TRAVELING & TRANSPORTATION

Car Maintenance

Keeping your car in a garage prolongs it's life and cuts down on mechanical problems because it isn't exposed to the elements. Highway driving is not hard on a car, short trips in traffic, where the engine doesn't warm up fully, is more damaging.

If your car breaks down on a highway, put your blinker on and pull off on the right hand shoulder. Open your hood and put on your flashers. If there isn't a safe place to stand, stay in the car with your seatbelt on because if someone hits your car, you want to be secure. If someone stops, ask them to call for help if you don't have a phone while you stay with the car.

Check your auto insurance for discounts on automatic seat belts, air bags, non-smokers or non-drinkers and anti-lock brakes. You did shop around for auto insurance, didn't you? Is your car worth less than $3000 or more than 6 years old? Drop your collision insurance because it is usually cheaper to fix the damage than to pay the yearly collision. Read your insurance policy to see how little it will cover.

Clear all the snow off your car in the winter. Don't drive with limited visibility. You are a hazard to other traffic. You are also advertising the fact you are a poor driver who doesn't care about the people around them. A blackboard eraser works well to clean the inside of your car's windows of condensation. Change your windshield wipers every 9 to 12 months. Take one into the store to make sure you get the right size and connecter.

Pamper your new car and avoid fast starts and stops to protect engine, transmission, clutch, and brakes. Vary the speed every 10 miles for the first 1000 miles. Do some highway driving to acclimate the engine. Let the engine warm up for a minute with your foot off the gas pedal, then start slowly. The engine usually warms up within 3 minutes. Change the oil every 3000 miles, the gas filter every 10,000 miles and the brake fluid every 24,000 miles or when your manual says. Keep tires properly inflated and aligned for safety's sake and save gas. Use cruise control, if you have it, on the highway. Keep your feet off the clutch and brake pedal when driving.

Don't overload your car. It isn't good for tires, reduces gas mileage, puts more strain on your transmission and engine, slows acceleration and braking times, and makes it harder to handle. Check tires often to make sure they are inflated correctly and are not excessively worn. Your life is riding on them. Plus you save money because underinflated tires lessen gas mileage.

There are many ways you may save money with your car. Use regular gas instead of premium. Learn to do simple car maintenance. On long car trips, pack meals and eat in rest areas. Look to see where the truckers are getting their gas because they usually know where the best prices are. And of course, buy a used car instead of a new one.

I never use a car wash. If the brushes are set to clean a small car, they will push the dirt into my larger car. And if the brushes are set to clean a big SUV, will they clean my car adequately? Here is how I wash my car. On a warm day I park in the shade. I fill one bucket with warm water and detergent, and another bucket with clear water. Using terrycloth towels, I first soap the entire car, then gently wash small sections starting at the top of the car. Then I rinse each section with clear water and finish by drying with a third towel. I never blast it with a hose on full because it would push the dirt into the paint.

The inside of the car windows I wash with a mixture of vinegar and water and dry with sections of newspaper. Yes, this gets the ink on my hands but newspaper does not leave little pieces of lint like paper towels do. And newspaper is cheaper.

Car Leaks

If you see something leaking, check the color, smell and feel. Don't taste anything. Gas has that familiar odor, antifreeze or coolant has a slight sweet smell and is usually green or yellow. Windshield washer fluid is bluish and smells like alcohol or detergent. Automatic transmission fluid and power steering fluid are red and oily. Grease is thick and sticky. Brake fluid is clear and watery and battery acid smells like sulfur.

Selling your Car

Don't do any major repairs, you usually won't get the money back. Get it cleaned inside and out, waxed, get the engine steam cleaned, tighten up anything loose or rattling and make any minor cosmetic repairs. It helps to have all service records to prove how well the car was taken care of. You can figure out a 'asking price' by checking online to see what similar cars are selling for or look up the value of your car in The Blue Book at the library. You can also drive it around to several car dealers and tell them you're thinking of selling and what would they offer. The highest price is probably close to your wholesale value. If you are going to trade it in on a new car, shop for the new car and get a purchase price in writing. Then discuss trading so the salesperson doesn't hike up the sales price. Bring in your old car to have the sales people appraise it.

If you are selling it yourself, write a short ad and stick in phrases that describe your car, like 'economical', 'well-maintained' or 'reliable'. Put the ad in car trading guides, local classifieds, and post it on the bulletin board in the college union. People expect to bargain your price down but don't drop more than $50 dollars at a time. Drop it $50 and let them come up $50 step by step. Only take cashier's checks or cash. Don't deal with minors because they can't be held to legal contracts. Sell it to their parents. On the day the title passes to the buyer, cancel the car insurance if you haven't done that already.

Renting a Car

If I Was Organized, I'd Be A Librarian

Ask yourself what fits your needs, not what you would like. Ask about discounts and extra charges, such as drop off, or extra mileage. Don't pay for extra insurance. Check your auto insurance policy to see if it covers a rental. Before you drive away, walk around and mark down any body damage (scrapes, dents, rust, etc.) on the rental form with the attendant. Test out lights, turn signals, horn, heater, air conditioner, radio, inside light. Note any non-working items on the form. If the license number isn't on the key chain, write it down to recognize it in a parking lot. Also write down the emergency service number because you might need it if the car is stolen or wrecked. Don't leave valuables in the car or trunk. Most rental cars are easy to spot. Automatic or late night drop offs require you to return all copies of the rental agreement so make a copy of the form before returning the car and mark down the final mileage on it. Don't pay the credit card charges until you get a copy of the rental form and you are sure the figures match. Dispute the bill if they don't and let your credit card company know about it before you pay. One place tried to gyp me out of a tank refill but with letters to them and to my credit company, they dropped that charge.

You know car rental firms sell their used cars to the public. My credit union even works with Enterprise Rent-A-Car to offer cars and car loans (at very low rates) to their members. The cars are usually one year old models and run the range from subcompacts up to commercial vans. The rental firms will give you the service report of everything that was done to the vehicle. Some even give you a test period in which to drive the car and will put that rental cost against the purchase price.

Car Accessories

I use an old briefcase as a carryall in my car. I strap it in the passenger seat and throw items in it. Maps, sunglasses, candy, stuff I'm bringing to friends, a small cassette recorder with a microphone so I can record notes when I am driving, camera and film, my wallet, spare change, and anything else I might want within reach.

In my car, I always carry maps, spare change, sunglasses, a bottle opener, a roll of paper towels, a paper bag for trash, a first aid kit under the front passenger's seat and a pair of binoculars. In the glove compartment I keep matches in a plastic bag, a small notebook, pens and pencils, a list of friend's and family's phone numbers (and another copy in my wallet), a plastic film can with aspirin and decongestants. I also have a hat, gloves, a rag or 2, and a piece of rope in the trunk along with tire changing equipment. In the winter I carry a blanket or sleeping bag.

In your traveling first aid kit you should have:
    tweezers and small scissors,
    pain relievers such as aspirin or acetaminophen,
    your prescription drugs (enough for the travel period),
    antacids, decongestants and antihistamines,
    diarrhea and motion sickness medicine,
    antiseptic and antibiotic ointment,
    bandages and gauze pads (or a roll of gauze) of various sizes, and medical tape,
    insect repellent, sunscreen,
    instant cold and hot compresses,
    and any other items you often need.

You can buy a traveler's first aid kit from your local Red Cross chapter or the AAA. Throw in a package of antiseptic baby wipes because they are useful to clean skin.

General Traveling Hints

Before you go traveling or on vacation, make lists. What has to be done before you go, what can wait until you return, and activities someone else can do. Let people know when you are going, especially those you work with and discuss any problems that might come up while you are not there. Check your camera if you haven't used it recently by shooting and developing a roll of film. Bring extra batteries and buy film and disposable cameras at home because they are more expensive at tourist areas. Going before or after the busy season can save plenty of money because you won't pay prime time rates on airfare and lodging. Check online for airfare bargains. Contact your state tourism bureau for info on activities to do close by. Some possibilities are state parks, festivals or fairs, museums, walking tours, historical sites. Buy the Sunday paper for a month and read the travel section to find local sites and activities. Ask your library for help and advice on local, statewide, national or international vacation ideas. Be flexible when traveling. You may save money by traveling at a different day or time.

When someone says they are going on a vacation or a business trip, ask them to bring you back maps, brochures, and tourist handouts from where they are going. Ask to see any pictures they took and ask what their impressions were. You will build up a file of info on places, get a good idea of what the place is like and what it would cost to visit. You will also learn more about that person. If your company has a library, ask them if they would collect travel materials from people to build up a travel file.

Put your suitcase and briefcase out several days before a trip so you can toss stuff in as you think of it. Keep a travel kit packed with items such as shaving needs, makeup, hair and nail care items, toothpaste & toothbrush, deodorant, comb & brush, pain relievers, etc. Use the small travel size of soap, shampoo, toothpaste, etc. I throw most items in a heavy-duty Ziploc plastic bag. Take 1 set of underwear for each day of the trip. Pack a pair of shoes for traveling, 1 formal set and an extra pair for walking. Choose outfits that can be worn in several combinations. Don't worry about wrinkles, you can't avoid them. Hanging clothes in the bathroom while you shower will get many wrinkles out.

Throw everything into a folder that concerns the trip; tickets, agendas, maps, timetables, phone numbers, etc. and keep it in one place for easy retrieval. Carry envelopes, business stationary, and stamps so you can write a quick note or a follow-up letter in your room or on the flight home and do it before you forget the facts and little details. A small dictaphone machine with microphone is very useful to record your ideas at anytime, anywhere. I use one when driving. It's safer to talk than write at 70 m.p.h. Carry a pocket size calendar to plan meetings, lunch and dinner appointments, note down facts about people (you make points when you email or call and wish someone happy birthday or anniversary). A laptop computer, modem, and fax machine are nice but it might be a bit of overkill on a pleasure trip.

Concerning luggage, keep track of what you really use and what your needs are. I get by with one large suitcase and my briefcase on business trips. On pleasure trips, it's one small suitcase, a shoulder bag or a small backpack. On camping trips, one backpack. I like something with many outside pockets to help me get items without digging thru the bag. If you buy a luggage carrier to wheel bags thru the airport and to the parking lot, it will pay for itself very soon. Every time you move, count your luggage to prevent you from leaving a piece in a plane, a cab, or in a hotel room. Wear sensible shoes. Save the fashion for dressy occasions and save your feet as you do all that walking.

While traveling, take some jobs to do in the airport or the plane. Bring notebooks, a calculator, pens and pencils, and perhaps your laptop computer. Listen to in-flight music to aid concentration or work thru the in-flight movie. Books on tape or self-improvement tapes are good, but you may get so interested in them you don't do any work.

Wear comfortable clothes that won't show wrinkles or stains too much. You know well enough to wear comfortable shoes as you will be doing lots of walking. In an airplane, after the doors close and you are ready to taxi, if you see several empty seats together, grab them so you can stretch out and nap. Don't overeat or drink much alcohol during the flight. The dry air dehydrates you and sitting in one position doesn't help digestion.

Drinks lots of water instead. Carry travelers checks (write down the numbers) instead of cash. Don't take expensive jewelry. Carry an extra pair of glasses. Leave an schedule with friends or family and check back in with them. Make a photocopy of your passport, driver's license, credit cards, and other papers and hide it among your clothing. If your wallet gets stolen or lost, you will need this to get replacements.

To get some exercise while traveling, lock your luggage into a locker and walk around the airport. Learn stretching exercises for legs, back and shoulders to combat the sitting you do. Pack a swimsuit and swim in the hotel pool or exercise in their exercise room. Walk up and down stairs instead of taking the elevator.

Keep a nomad mentality when traveling by maintaining a sense of wonder about the world around you, keeping an open mind, and being flexible and friendly.

Leaving your car at the airport or bus or train station while you go on a short trip? Put money, $10 or $20, in an envelope under a floor mat for emergency purposes when you return.

Business Travel

As soon as I know I'm going to a conference or meeting, I use business cards collected from earlier meetings to call up fun people and make arrangements for lunch and dinner dates, drinks, sight-seeing, and so on. This keeps me from spending evenings channel surfing the television in the hotel. Of course I leave one or two evenings open for relaxing and chance encounters.

I wear my conference badge on my right side so when someone is shaking my hand, they can easily see my name badge. Improve meetings you attend by planning how to work them. Develop a short self-introduction, "Hello, I'm Dale and I help people get organized.", that will help people remember you. Focus on the positive benefits you are getting by attending, such as meeting people who will be helpful in business. Carry enough business cards to give to people, but ask yourself if you really want this person to call you. If so, ask for one of theirs and give one of yours. If they don't have one, cross off the info on yours and have them write on the back. Crossing off your name will prevent you from giving that card away.

Carry a business card organizer (available from office supply stores) and go over it on the way to the meeting or conference. Everyone will think you have a good memory when you mention something about them you heard and wrote down on their card.

Traveling at night saves the cost of a hotel room. Usually hotels in the center of town are more expensive than ones outside town. Ask for the room rate before signing in to make sure the advertised rate applies to the room you are getting. Call both the hotel and the toll-free reservation number and take the best price offered. Ask for what you want in a room: quiet, safety, an outlet for your computer modem, or a view. Complain right away when you find something wrong. You might ask to see 2 or 3 rooms and choose between them. Book a room near the elevator or the stairs for safety. Make sure your room has a peephole and more than one door lock. Pay with a credit card so you can complain to your card company in case of a dispute. Always check the bills carefully for overcharges. If you don't charge anything to the room, it's easy to spot any extra items that aren't yours. Leave a tip for the hotel cleaning staff every day. This will get you better service than leaving a tip on the last day of your stay. Guarantee your room for late arrival so delayed flights won't be a problem. Call the local convention bureau for help instead of always relying on the hotel for information. Go down early the morning you are leaving and checkout before checkout time. You will avoid the rush and still have the use of your room.

I always ask the hotel staff if they were going to take their family out to eat locally, where would they go. I tell them my company limits what I spend each day on meals so I want a good meal at a good price and I would like to stay away from any restaurant chains. I have found some great local food this way.

Oh yes, remember the antiseptic wipes I suggested you carry in your car? Bring some along on your travels too and use them to wipe the television remote control and the telephone in your hotel room.

A FEW MORE WORDS

Did I suggest separating your work clothes from your play clothes to make it easier to find items or get dressed? Did I suggest reading the various newspaper columns giving tips on finance, housework, career, travel, etc., and saving them in folders? Did I suggest asking your friends how they stay organized and using their ideas?

There are so many ideas on self-organization that one book can not hold them all. There is no one right way to be organized. What works for me might not work for you. All I hope is this book has given you some ideas and will help start some habits which improve your life.

Nowhere in my education, except during the `bullsh*t' sessions in the Army and in college, did anyone ever talk about their purpose in life. What is yours? Do you remember how important forgiveness and gratitude is? If you focus on the good things in life, life is enjoyable. If you focus on the bad things, life isn't. No cosmic truth here.

At the monthly meetings of the Black Widowers, the question put to any guest is "How do you justify your existence?" Well, HOW DO YOU?

NEVER (using your discretion) pass up the opportunity to hug or be hugged, kiss or be kissed, take a trip, go to a party, or do activities you have never done before. Laugh at yourself. Accept your mistakes. If you aren't making any, you aren't doing anything. Admit it was your mistake. Apologize. Review what and where you went wrong. Do the correct action and remember it for the next time. You can have almost anything, but not everything, you want. And if you did get everything you want, where would you keep it?

Now if you will excuse me, I've put off cleaning while finishing indexing this book and my place is a mess.

Have fun.

Where to find these or other books on these subjects? Ask your local librarians. Browse through the ENTIRE section they point out to you. Read the covers, open the book and look at the table of contents and the index. If it grabs your curiosity, borrow it or at least sit down and browse through it. Then, if you decide it's a great book, go buy your own copy.

HUMAN POTENTIAL

Ailes, Roger 'You Are the Message' Dow Jones Irwin
Bandler, Richard 'Using Your Brain For A Change' Real People Press
Brown, David 'The Rest of Your Life is the Best of Your Life: David Brown's Guide to Growing Gray (Disgracefully)' Barricade Books
Cialdini, Robert B. 'Influence: The Psychology of Persuasion' William Morrow
Cypert, Samuel A. 'Believe and Achieve: W. Clement Stone's 17 Principles of Success' Avon Books
Greene, James and Lewis, David 'Know Your Own Mind: Nine Tests That Tell You What You Do Best' Rawson Associates
Haas, Robert 'Eat Smart, Think Smart' HarperCollins Publishers
Heinlein, Robert 'The Notebooks of Lazarus Long' Pomegranate Artbooks
Inamori, Kazuo 'A Passion for Success: Practical, Inspirational, and Spiritual Insight from Japan's Leading Entrepreneur' McGraw-Hill
Konner, Melvin 'Why the Reckless Survive' Penguin Books
Kushel, Gerald 'Effective Thinking for Uncommon Success' Amacom
Oldham, John M. and Morris, Lois B. 'The Personality Self-Portrait: Why You Think, Work, Love, and Act the Way You Do' Bantam Books
Peck, M. Scott 'The Road Less Traveled' Simon and Schuster
Ringer, Robert J. 'Looking Out for #1' Fawcett Crest
Staples, Walter Doyle 'Think Like a Winner', Pelican Publishing

von Oech, Roger 'A Kick In The Seat Of The Pants' Harper & Row

Winter, Arthur and Winter, Ruth 'Build Your Brain Power' St. Martin's Press

Waitley, Dennis 'The New Dynamics of Winning' William Morrow and Company

HOUSE/HOME

Better Homes and Gardens 'Household Hints and Tips' Dorling Kindersley

Cuppy, Will 'How to Be a Hermit' or 'A Bachelor Keeps House' Liveright Publishing

Heloise 'Heloise from A to Z' Perigee Books

Heloise 'Heloise Hints for All Occasions' Perigee Books

Japikse, Carl 'The $1.98 Cookbook: How to Eat Like a Gourmet and Save $6,000 a Year' Enthea Press

Marsh, Dorothy B., editor 'Good Housekeeping Cookbook' Good Housekeeping Book Division

MONEY

Clifford, Denis 'Plan Your Estate: Wills, Probate Avoidance, Trusts & Taxes' Nolo Press

Givens, Charles J. 'Financial Self-Defense' Simon and Schuster

Lynch, Peter 'One Up on Wall Street: How to Use What You Know to Make Money in the Market' Simon and Schuster

McAleese, Tama 'Get Rich Slow' Career Press

McAleese, Tama 'Money: How to Get it, Keep it and Make it Grow' Career Press

Phillips, Michael 'The Seven Laws of Money' Random House

Phillips, Michael 'Simple Living Investments' Clear Glass Publishing

Pollan, Stephen M. 'Die Broke: A Radical, Four-Part Financial Plan' HarperBusiness

Pugsley, John A. 'The Alpha Strategy: The Ultimate Plan of Financial Self-Defense' Stratford Press

Ringer, Robert J. 'Million Dollar Habits' Fawcett Crest

Terhorst, Paul 'Cashing in on the American Dream: How to Retire at 35' Bantam

BUDGET CATEGORIES:

food
        food at home
        food away from home

housing
        mortgage or rent
        utilities, services, and fuels
         electricity or gas
         telephone
        household operations and supplies
        household equipment and furnishings
        home insurance

clothes: sort by men, women, and children

transportation
        vehicle purchases
        gas and oil
        maintenance and repairs
        vehicle inspection and registration
        public transportation

health care
        health insurance
        medical services

personal insurance and pensions
        life and personal insurance
        pensions and social security

personal care products

reading and education

entertainment
        television, radio, music, sound equipment
        fees and admissions

alcoholic beverages and tobacco products

miscellaneous

If I Was Organized, I'd Be A Librarian

Camping Equipment List:

clothes:	underwear
	socks
	shirt
	trousers
	belt
	hiking boots and camp shoes
	handkerchief(s)
	hat(s)
	jacket(s) - pile, down, vapor-barrier, wind
	long pant(s) - pile, down, vapor-barrier,
wind	
	vest
	long johns
	sweater
	shorts
	rain jacket, rain pants, and poncho
	gloves
	swimsuit
house:	tent with waterproof ground cloth, poles,
pegs	
	sleeping bag
	foam pad or air mattress
	space blanket
kitchen:	canteen
	cook kit: pots, pans
	knife, fork, spoon
	stove and fuel
	matches in waterproof container
	salt, pepper, sugar, other spices
	can opener
	dish cloth, dish towel
	soap for cleaning pots and pans

water purification tablets

equipment: first aid kit
flashlight, batteries, and spare bulb
candles
lantern and fuel
glasses and sunglasses
binoculars
camera and lots of film
maps
compass
towel
soap
toothbrush and toothpaste
comb or brush
toilet paper in waterproof plastic bag
insect repellant
suntan lotion
matches in waterproof container
whistle
rope and nylon cord
notebook and writing implements
watch
thermometer
tent and pack repair kits
needles and thread
spare plastic bags
clothespins
space blanket

Car Equipment List:

    engine oil, 2 quarts
    water, 1 gallon
    spare tire in good condition
    tire pressure gauge
    car jack and tire iron for removing tire
    cleaning rags
    road safety kit with flares and 'help' sign
    paper towels
    maps
    first aid kit
    bottle of pain reliever in glove compartment
    flashlight
    spare fuses
    small tool kit: pliers, screwdriver, knife, etc.
    blanket or sleeping bag
    citizen's band (CB) radio
    radar detector
    cellular phone
    sunglasses

FRUIT & VEGETABLES
apples
bananas
beets
broccoli
carrots
celery
chickpeas
chives
corn
cucumber
garlic
grapefruit
green beans
leeks
lettuce
melons
mushrooms
onions
oranges
pears
peas
peppers
potatoes
spinach
squash
string beans
sweet potatoes
tomatoes
turnips
zucchini

DAIRY
butter
cheese:
        cheddar
        cottage
        grated Parmesan
        gouda
        Muenster
        ricotta
eggs
milk: fat free
sour cream
yogurt: fat free plain

CONDIMENTS & SPICES
baking powder
baking soda
basil
bay leaf
broth: chicken, beef, vegetable
chili powder
chives
cinnamon
cooking oil: bottle, spray
dill
garlic powder
gravy: beef, chicken, turkey
horseradish
hot sauce
ketchup
lemon juice
limejuice
mayonnaise
mustard: brown, yellow, Dijon
non-sugar substitute
olive oil
oregano
paprika
parsley
pepper
rosemary
salad dressing
salt
soy sauce
teriyaki sauce
thyme
Worcestershire sauce

MEATS
bacon
burger
chicken
cold cuts
fish
hot dogs
kielbasa
pork chops
pot roast
roast beef
sausage
Spam
spiced ham
steak
stew beef
turkey

MISCELLANEOUS FOOD
applesauce
beans
        black, garbanzo
        lentils, red kidney
bird food
chili
clams & clam sauce
cranberry sauce
crushed tomatoes
flour
green peas dried
gum
honey
jam or jelly
Marsala wine
milk: condensed, evaporated
nuts
olives: green, black
peanut butter
pickles
pork-n-beans
sardines
sauerkraut
soup:
        chicken noodle
        clam chowder
        cream of mushroom
        tomato
sugar: brown, white
syrup
tomato paste
tuna
vinegar: regular, apple cider

FROZEN FOOD
breakfast sausage
piecrust
pizza
sorbet
waffles
vegetables:
        broccoli
        Brussels sprouts
        carrots
        corn
        green beans
        peas
        spinach

If I Was Organized, I'd Be A Librarian

BEVERAGES
coffee: decaf, regular
juice:
    apple
    cranberry
    grape
    grapefruit
    orange
    tomato or V*
lemonade
seltzer
tea: black, green, PG Tips
tonic water

BREAD
bagels
bread: rye, wheat, white
breadcrumbs
crackers
English muffins
stuffing

CEREAL
cold cereal
Cream of Wheat
Farina
grits
oatmeal
wheat germ

PASTA
couscous
egg noodles
elbows
frozen pasta dinners
lasagna
rice: brown, white
spaghetti
spaghetti sauce

PAPER PRODUCTS
aluminum foil
coffee filters
oven cooking bags
paper plates
paper towels
plastic storage bags
    freezer
    large
    sandwich size
plastic wrap
tissues
toilet paper
trash bags
water filters
wax paper

PERSONAL ITEMS
allergy & nose drops
antacid
antihistamine: Zyrtec
aspirin
baby wipes
band-aids
conditioner
contact lens cleaning solution
cotton balls
cough drops
deodorant
ibuprofen
lactate tablets
melatonin
Q-tips
razor blades
shampoo: dandruff, regular
shoe polish
soap: bath, hand
tampons & liners
tooth floss
toothbrush
toothpaste
vitamins

CLEANING ITEMS & MISC
air freshener
all purpose cleaner
ammonia
bleach
Bon Ami
candles
dish detergent
dishwasher soap
Drano
dryer sheets
laundry detergent
liquid hand soap
Lysol cleanser
Lysol all purpose wipes
oven cleaner
Shout laundry spray
Soft Scrub cleaner
SOS pads
sponges
spray freshener
Spray-n-Wash
tile cleaner
toilet bowl cleaner
vacuum cleaner bags
Windex
Woollite

If I Was Organized, I'd Be A Librarian

The two previous pages show what my shopping list looks like when it is printed out on a 8" x 10" sheet of paper. Since that is not the size of this book, I will now give you the food categories so you may copy them into your computer, modify them according to your needs, wants, likes and dislikes, and print out the food shopping list to keep on your fridge.

FRUIT & VEGETABLES
apples
bananas
beets
broccoli
carrots
celery
chickpeas
chives
corn
cucumber
garlic
grapefruit
green beans
leeks
lettuce
melons
mushrooms
onions
oranges
pears
peas
peppers
potatoes
spinach
squash
string beans
sweet potatoes
tomatoes
turnips
zucchini

If I Was Organized, I'd Be A Librarian

DAIRY
butter
cheese:
    cheddar
    cottage
    Feta
    grated Parmesan
    gouda
    Muenster
    ricotta
eggs
milk: fat free
sour cream
yogurt: fat free plain

CONDIMENTS & SPICES
baking powder
baking soda
basil
bay leaf
broth: chicken, beef, vegetable
chili powder
chives
cinnamon
cooking oil: bottle, spray
dill
garlic powder
gravy: beef, chicken, turkey
horseradish
hot sauce
ketchup
lemon juice
lime juice
mayonnaise
mustard: brown, yellow, Dijon
non-sugar substitute
olive oil

oregano
paprika
parsley
pepper
rosemary
salad dressing
salt
soy sauce
teriyaki sauce
thyme
Worcestershire sauce

MEATS
bacon
burger
chicken
cold cuts
fish
hot dogs
kielbasa
pork chops
pot roast
roast beef
sausage
Spam
spiced ham
steak
stew beef
turkey

MISCELLANEOUS FOOD
applesauce
beans
        black, garbanzo, lentils, red kidney
chili
clams & clam sauce
cranberry sauce

crushed tomatoes
flour
green peas dried
gum
honey
jam or jelly
Marsala wine
milk: condensed, evaporated
nuts
olives: green, black
peanut butter
pickles
pork-n-beans
sardines
sauerkraut
soup:
    chicken noodle
    clam chowder
    cream of mushroom
    tomato
sugar: brown, white
syrup
tomato paste
tuna
vinegar: regular, apple cider, red wine,

FROZEN FOOD
breakfast sausage
hash brown potatoes
piecrust
pizza
sorbet
waffles
vegetables:
    broccoli
    Brussels sprouts
    carrots
    corn

peas
spinach

BEVERAGES
coffee: decaf, regular
juice:
        apple
        cranberry
        grape
        grapefruit
        orange
        tomato or V8
lemonade
seltzer
tea: black, green, PG Tips
tonic water

BREAD
bagels
bread: rye, wheat, white
breadcrumbs
crackers
English muffins
stuffing

CEREAL
cold cereal
Cream of Wheat
Farina
grits
oatmeal
wheat germ

PASTA
couscous

egg noodles
elbows
lasagna
rice: brown, white
spaghetti
spaghetti sauce

PAPER PRODUCTS
aluminum foil
coffee filters
oven cooking bags
paper plates
paper towels
plastic storage bags
      freezer
      large
      sandwich size
plastic wrap
tissues
toilet paper
trash bags
water filters
wax paper

PERSONAL ITEMS
allergy & nose drops
antacid
antihistamine: Zyrtec
aspirin
baby wipes
band-aids
conditioner
contact lens cleaning solution
cotton balls
cough drops
deodorant
ibuprofen

If I Was Organized, I'd Be A Librarian

lactate tablets
melatonin
Q-tips
razor blades
shampoo: dandruff, regular
shoe polish
soap: bath, hand
tampons & liners
tooth floss
toothbrush
toothpaste
vitamins

CLEANING ITEMS & MISC
air freshener
all purpose cleaner
ammonia
bleach
Bon Ami
Brillo pads
candles
dish detergent
dishwasher soap
Drano
dryer sheets
laundry detergent
liquid hand soap
Lysol cleanser
Lysol all purpose wipes
oven cleaner
Shout laundry spray
Soft Scrub cleaner
SOS pads
sponges
spray freshener
Spray-n-Wash
tile cleaner
toilet bowl cleaner

vacuum cleaner bags
Windex
Woolite

FAMILY GIFT FORM

Name:
Size: Shirt/blouse   Pants   Shoes

Color of: Kitchen   Bedroom
             Living Room   Bathroom

What is your favorite?
    Color
    Movie
    Type of Music
    Musical Group/Artist
    Book/Author
    Food   Drink
    Restaurant
    Brand Name (Clothes)
    Cartoon Character
    TV Show
    Actor/Actress

Favorite Team and Player:
    Baseball   Basketball
    Football   Hockey
    Soccer   Other

Hobbies/Collectibles

Do You Own: DVD/VCR   CD
    Computer (Model, etc.)
    Videogame

Three Most Wanted Gifts:
    1.
    2.
    3.

Unneeded or unwanted gifts:

Any Occasion Gift List:
- a silly picture of you and your family
- a non-silly picture of you and your family
- extension cords with surge suppressors
- fire extinguishers
- fire safe to store valuable papers
- plastic storage boxes of various sizes with snap-on tops
- picture frames of various sizes
- assorted candles of various sizes and scents
- reference books: an atlas, real good dictionary, Guinness Book of World Records, books on local birds, insects, animals, flowers, and trees
- magazine subscriptions: National Geographic, Consumer Reports, Kiplinger Personal Finance Magazine, any in the areas or activities that person is interested in
- sports equipment for sports anyone can play, such as Frisbees, water pistols, sidewalk chalk, and bubble makers,
- The Old Farmer's Almanac

New Apartment or House Gift Items:
  cleaning: plastic bucket, mop, broom and dustpan, sponges, scrub brush, rags and paper towels, waste baskets, trash bags,

  tool kit: hammer, pliers, screwdrivers, flashlights, measuring tape, scissors, knife, assorted nails, screws and bolts, tape (duct, clear, electrical, etc.), electrical drill and drill bits, saber saw and blades, circular saw and blades, paintbrushes and paint pan, handsaw,
- lawn tools: lawn mower, rake, broom, shovels
- extension cords with surge suppressors
- batteries of various sizes
- fan(s)
- lamps and light bulbs
- clock(s)
- thumbtacks
- notepaper and writing implements
- stepstool or stepladder
- calendar

INDEX

appointment calendar	10
automobile	57
bar, stocking	55
bills, handling	17
budgeting	27
car accessories	60, 73
choice making	5
chores, household	11
cleaning	14
clothespins	4
clothing, buying	52
Consumer Reports	30
coupons	12
credit cards	28
debts, attacking	26
dress, style of	52
energy level	22
expenses, types of	26
financial well-being	26
finding items	33
folders	8
food shopping	11, 61
gift buying	63, 64
'Gotta wanna'	7
house & home	37
household chores	11
ideas, finding	32
laundry	15
libraries	4, 58
lists, making	7
living areas, four	40
magazines	18, 36
mail, handling	17
memory	33
money	25
money pie	26
moving	42

newspapers	33
notebook	7
organization, folders for	8, 18
organization, purpose of	4
packing to move	43
packrat collecting	8
paper	17
party, planning	54
priority ranking	5
procrastination	23
purpose of being organized	4
renting a car	60
retirement	27
sale times	30
self-improvement tapes	64
shopping, food	11
shopping, lists	13, 29, 61
social activities	50
telephone	51
television, turn off	50
time management	19
to-do list	7
travel	61
viewpoints	35
what to do first	5
work area	9
write it down	35

www.ingramcontent.com/pod-product-compliance
Lightning Source LLC
Chambersburg PA
CBHW020017050426
42450CB00005B/522